MW01172900

Things I Learned About

Angels

Things I Learned About

Angels

John Barton Gross

Copyright © 2023 by John Barton Gross

No part of this publication may be reproduced, stored in a retrieval system, or transmitted in any form or by any means, electronic, mechanical, photocopying, recording, or otherwise, without the written consent of the author.

All rights reserved.

ISBN: 979-8-218-18526-8 (Paperback)
ISBN 979-8-218-20338-2 (Ebook)

Library of Congress Control Number 2023907188

Scripture taken from the New King James Version®. Copyright © 1982 by Thomas Nelson. Used by permission. All rights reserved.

Cover design by Bryson Allen at bryallendesigns.com

Published by John Barton Gross
nightpilot300@yahoo.com

Printed in the United States of America

Linda,

John Luke,

Sara Beth, Heather, and Haley

For He shall give His angels charge over
you,
To keep you in all your ways.

Psalms 91:11

CONTENTS

PREFACE

The air was cool and crisp one December evening as I eased my way from my hunting blind and started my walk out of the woods and towards my home. The sky was crystal clear as I rounded the corner of a field next to the Yockanookany River and out into the open pasture that I had crossed many times on evenings just like this one. The Sun had set, and the stars were beginning to shine. It is one of my favorite times of the day, and one of my favorite places to be. We all have that place. That place where we can go to find peace and solitude. As I stood in the middle of that pasture, I was in my place. All around me, I could see the sky. From horizon to horizon, stars spread over me like an umbrella. There was nothing but stars and the quiet of the moment, and in that quiet was conversation. As I walk out of the woods, my habit is to talk to the Lord, typically thanking Him for all that He is and all that He has done for me. Invariably as I get to this place in my walk, surrounded by His magnificent creation, the conversation turns to my time of wondering. I have always believed that my Father in Heaven has never minded nor shied away from the questions that originate in my curious mind. This night was no different.

I had recently put the finishing touches on a study I wrote for my Sunday school class on the topic of Heaven. My thoughts lately had been on how magnificent Heaven was going to be with all the wonderful things I had been thinking so much of over the past several months. Then I started to think about how much of Heaven we must know nothing about. What else has God created that He has not told us about? I could almost hear the Lord laugh as if to say, *"You'll just have to wait and find out."*

Then I thought about the angels. Surely Heaven will be full of angels. What do they look like? What do they do? When I get to heaven, how will I interact with them? I mean, will we sit down and talk, or will they be busy doing angel stuff? Who are they anyway and why am I here on earth, and they are in Heaven?

I concluded, that there is no way to learn about the things that God has created that He has chosen not to tell us about. However, He has chosen to give us some insight into angels. After all, the Bible is full of references to angels. So, my journey began. My lust for knowledge and my desire to know more about my Lord started me thinking about angels. If God created them, and they are in Heaven surrounding His throne, then they must be very special. I wanted to know more about them.

I have researched enough other topics to know that there are some good books out there in which to learn things like this, but there are far more that are simply one person's opinion. There are very few opinions out there worth investing my time in, so I concentrated my research in the one book I knew would give me the straight answers I was looking for, the Bible.

The chapters that follow are what I learned. I am by no means an angel expert and do not claim to be one. Although I have a couple of degrees, none of them relate to anything having to do with angels or theology. I am simply a layman, a child of God with a desire to know Him more intimately. With the Bible as my guide and a careful selection of references, I have collected answers to most of my questions. This is by no means a fully exhaustive book on angels. Rather, it is a book that I am sure will give you a broad understanding of angels and answer many of the common questions people have about them. I pray that as you read through the pages of this little book you too will find answers to questions that you may have about angels. I also pray that as you learn more about the angelic world, you will be drawn closer to God. After all, drawing closer to God is what this life is all about. So, sit down, relax, and enjoy reading the things I learned about angels.

ACKNOWLEDGEMENTS

Along this road called life, we all have people that influence us and lend a small hand in the making of who we are and eventually into what we do. Most of these people have no knowledge of the impact they make. In my life, there have been many that made an impact, from high school math, science, and band teachers, you know who you are; to leaders of my Royal Ambassador group at church, you also know who you are. I have always tried to take a small piece of those influential people with me to enhance my life, and to those who have allowed me to do that, I say thank you.

Each week I get the pleasure of standing before a great group of people that allow me the pleasure of leading their Sunday School class. It is because of them that works like this have taken shape. It is because of this great class that I have not only studied the Bible, but have written down the things I have learned. Some of those things coalesced into what you will read here. To the wonderful friends of this class and our entire church family that allow me to teach and learn, I say thank you. 777

I would like to thank the many people who helped in proofing the manuscript for this book. Your keen eye for the details and your rich knowledge of God's word were invaluable in making this book what it is.

To Stephen Evans, my paster and friend, thank you brother for all you are. 777

A special thank you goes to my wife for loving and encouraging me along this path. She is the rock and foundation of our family. It is her never ending, unselfish love that makes life so wonderful. To her, with a hug and a kiss, I say thank you for all you are to me and our family.

And most importantly, a special thank you to my Lord and Savior. Thank you for the unending curiosity that you have placed inside me to learn more about you and your wonderful creation. Thank you for loving me so much that you gave your own life so that I could spend eternity in your loving presence. Thank you for blessing this work so that it may touch the lives of those who read it.

PART ONE

AN OVERVIEW OF ANGELS

CHAPTER ONE

BELIEF IN ANGELS

Since the beginning of time, man has been curious about many things. My life has been filled with curiosity. It is not enough for me to know that something exists. I want to know how it works, what its function is, and why it exists. It has never been enough for me to simply look at the stars and wonder at their beauty. Oh, I do that, but more often, I am thinking of the physics that makes them so beautiful. I once had an elderly gentleman neighbor that referred to it as my lust for knowledge. This same lust for knowledge or curiosity by mankind has led to many fascinating discoveries that have spawned the invention of almost every modern-day convenience that we have. It seems that as we look around our Lord's awesome universe there is no shortage of things to be curious about.

One of the things that I have learned, through discussions with people on the topic of heaven, is that they are curious about angels. If you are reading this book, then you probably share that curiosity. Angels are throughout the Bible and a part of our lives, but we know little about them.

This curiosity that we humans have about angels is so widespread and never-ending that it has a name. Scholars call it Angelology.

Angelology, or the study of angels, has been with us since the very first angel appeared to man. Historically, it has been simply a study of angels to learn more about them so that we can have an accurate representation of yet another of God's wonderful creatures. Today, however, it appears to have become its own religion filled with books, paintings, and little angels that sit on our shelves. Walk into any store that sells little trinkets and you'll find little winged angels sitting on shelves or hanging on things.

You probably have several angels like that in your house. Now, there is nothing wrong with having little angels around your house. One sits atop our Christmas tree every December. Several even sit on our shelves. The problem for some is that it is more than just little angels sitting on shelves.

Magazines, books, and television shows have even joined in the angel craze. *Guidepost* magazine is one of the more popular Christian magazines, and publishes a separate bi-monthly magazine called *Angels on Earth* which has more than a million subscribers. People simply love to read stories of modern-day angel activity.

In the early '90s, angel mania took off with books and T.V. shows. Shows like "Touched by an Angel" and "Highway to Heaven" were watched every week by people from all walks of life, each dreaming of having their own angelic experience. Folks everywhere were talking about experiences with angels. Angel stuff was everywhere. Some of it was good stuff, but most of it was simply things born of man's imagination.

Even today you must be careful about the books you read on angels. I did a search on Amazon for books about angels and stopped counting at 30. Some of those books seemed legitimate, but many were not. Several books that I have read in doing my research have been good, but many that I looked at were more along the lines of new-age spiritualism.

One author talked about an angel that spent almost every day with her. It would show up whenever she called and would even find parking places for her. It was her parking lot angel. That might sound like a handy thing to have, but somehow, I doubt it is very biblical.

So, is all this interest in Angels good or bad? Well, like anything else I suppose that it has both good and bad sides.

Anything that causes us to concentrate more on the things of God is a good thing in my book. It could be that God is using our interest in angels to prepare our minds for things to come. He could be using our curiosity about angels to give us hope for a future in a place that is so wonderful that our minds cannot even imagine. After all, we as Christians long for the day when we step into eternity and enter heaven to be with our Lord and all our loved ones. In that place there will be angels. Because of that, it is only natural to be curious about what they will be like.

Indeed, anything that causes us to concentrate more on the things of God is a good thing. However, it is also true that anything that causes us to be distracted from God is bad. Sometimes Satan even uses the good things in life to distract us from God. In the case of angels, it could be said that Satan is using them to distract us from the one true God. If Satan could replace God with angels and get people to love and focus on them instead of God, he could get lots of people to forget entirely about God. That's exactly what a lot of people have done. They have adopted angels in place of God because their angels don't require anything from them. This phenomenon has even been referred to as "God Lite." It is having the satisfaction of a spiritual being looking over oneself without the biblical restrictions of God limiting the fun that this world offers.

Having said all of that, the issue of angelology is not in itself bad. To say so, would be like saying that physics was bad. After all, physics is the reason for the atomic bomb that killed thousands in World War II. Yet, it is also what has given us the light bulb, telephone, and countless other useful things in life.

Remember, angelology is simply the study of angels. Like physics, it is what we do with the information gathered that becomes bad. Just as physics has led to many useful things in life, angelology can lead us to a greater understanding of God and His creation. After all, thats what this book is all about. Since we will be spending eternity with angels, wouldn't it be nice to know a little about them?

Before we begin our journey into learning about angels, there is one very important point that we need to address. That point, is the belief in angels.

I recently read a study that said that only eighty-eight percent of Christians in America believe in angels. How can you be a Christian and not believe in angels? For some it is easy. After all, you have probably never seen one and the things you have heard about and will read about here may seem like some made-up science fiction story. I readily admit that some facts that you are soon to read about angels seem rather far out there. Don't let this discourage you from continuing down this road of learning. It was only a few years ago when having a device that we could not only communicate on; but take pictures on, gather information from unlimited resources with, and multitask hundreds of other chores was reserved for Star Trek. Now almost every person alive carries a smartphone capable of all of that and more. When the technology experts tell us of the new advances headed our way, we don't doubt them, we look forward to the next gee-whiz gadget with great anticipation. So why do we not do the same with the Word of God?

With smartphones and high-tech gadgets in everyone's pockets, there is no doubt that we live in the "Information Age." One can learn about any topic he or she wishes simply by logging onto the internet. If you need information for a school report, simply log on. If you want to learn how to tweak the engine of your 1994 F150 pickup, simply log on. If the internet does not fill your void for knowledge, then walk through any of the big-box bookstores, and you can find books on subjects from relationships to goldfish. You can even find books on angels. But there is only one book that we can say with confidence holds the answers that we truly seek. That book is the Bible.

The Bible is completely accurate and infallible in every way. It is the very words of our Lord. Look at a few verses that tell us over and over that the information in the Bible is true and accurate.

For the word of God is living and powerful, and sharper than any two-edged sword, piercing even to the division of soul and spirit, and of joints and marrow, and is a discerner of the thoughts and intents of the heart.

Hebrews 4:12

And so we have the prophetic word con-firmed, which you do well to heed as a light that shines in a dark place until the day dawns and the morning star rises in your hearts; knowing this first, that no prophecy of Scripture is of any private interpretation, for prophecy never came by the will of man, but holy men of God spoke as they were moved by the Holy Spirit.

2 Peter 1:19-21

All Scripture is given by inspiration of God, and is profitable for doctrine, for reproof, for correction, for instruction in righteousness, that the man of God may be complete, thoroughly equipped for every good work.

2 Timothy 3:16-17

*The law of the LORD is perfect, converting the soul;
The testimony of the LORD is sure, making wise the simple;*

Psalm 19:7

*The words of the LORD are pure words,
Like silver tried in a furnace of earth,
Purified seven times.*

Psalms 12:6

*Every word of God is pure;
He is a shield to those who put their trust in Him.*

Proverbs 30:5

Sanctify them by Your truth. Your word is truth.

John 17:17

One version of the Bible tells us in 2 Timothy 3:16 that God simply breathed out all of creation. If we are indeed searching to learn more about the angelic creations of God, there's no better place to turn than the creator's word.

If we were to look at an original manuscript of the Bible, we would find that we would need to be able to read Hebrew and Greek. If we were so blessed to be able to do that, we could find in our Bible two words, "Malak" and "Angelos". Both words translate to our English word "angel". Malak is the Hebrew word for angel and Angelos is the Greek. In both Hebrew and Greek, the word for angel means "messenger".

From Genesis to Revelation, we find references to these messengers whom we call angels. There are references to angels in thirty-four of the sixty-six books of the Bible. Altogether, there are over 300 references to angels in scripture. We find these references to angels more times in the Bible than we do the word sin.

To give you an idea of how important the topic of angels is in the Bible, simply look at the New Testament, and you will find more references to angels than to love. Matthew, Mark, Luke, and John all speak of angels in their works. All four of the gospel writers tell of angels at Jesus' tomb the morning that Mary found it empty. The book of Revelation mentions angels more than sixty-five times throughout its explanation of the end times. All these references make it clear that the Bible has much to say concerning angels.

The writers of the Bible leave little doubt about their belief in angels, but what about your belief in angels? After all, you probably have never seen one, and therefore, must take it by faith that they exist. This question of belief in angels falls into the same category as our belief in Noah's Ark, talking donkeys, men rising from the dead, an entire population one day simply disappearing, and a love so great that a man would sacrifice Himself on a Roman cross.

It is easy to believe in things that you have seen with your own eyes, but it is what you have not seen and still believe in that will ultimately matter. Jesus said so Himself when He appeared to His disciples after His resurrection. Thomas finally believed that Jesus had truly risen from the dead. Listen to what Jesus said to Thomas.

Have you believed because you have seen me? Blessed are those who have not seen and yet have believed.

John 20:29

"Blessed are those who have not seen and yet have believed". For some, this is a real issue. Many like to pick and choose the things in scripture to believe or not to believe. I suppose it makes them feel better about themselves. Once, I was having a conversation with a man who claims to have a devout belief in Jesus Christ and all the things taught in the gospels. The subject of our conversation revolved around the belief of things in the Bible. I simply mentioned that I believe in the Bible as it is written. His response was, "You mean to tell me that you actually believe that two of every creature came from all over the world and got on a boat built by some old man." My answer was an emphatic yes. Yes, I believe that two of every creature came from all over the world and got on a boat built by some old man. Not only that, but I also believe that once that happened, God sealed them inside and it rained for forty days and forty nights flooding the entire Earth. I believe that and several other things that I have not seen. Why? Because my Bible tells me that the things in it happened or are going to happen. As the old saying goes, "the Bible says it and that settles it."

I don't know where you stand on this matter, but let me say this; you cannot pick and choose what to believe from God's word. You either believe the Bible or you don't. By that, I mean the entire Bible. One must take the word of God as a whole. It cannot be broken down into bits and pieces of our choosing, doing so belittles what God has to say. Not only that, but it is arrogant of the created to be assigning fact and fiction to things given by the creator Himself. If one testifies that they have faith in God, then one must also have faith in the things God felt important enough to tell us of in His word.

So, ask yourself, do you believe the word of God? If the answer is yes, then there leaves no doubt as to the existence of angels. If in fact after all the references to angels the Bible contains and one still does not believe in the existence of angels, then one must question whether one believes the Bible or not.

CHAPTER TWO

CREATED BEINGS

What are angels? On the surface that seems like an easy question to answer. However, when you get right down to answering it, one may find that angels are as complicated a creation as humans are. Not to mention the fact that we don't have the full picture of angels. For some reason, God has allowed us to know of angels and has involved them in our lives as is evident in the Bible, but He has chosen not to reveal the full story to us. After all, He is God. In His infinite wisdom, He has decided that only a portion of the story is all that we need. For some, just knowing that angels exist settles it. But if you are reading this book, then you are like me and want to know more than that. So, let's start at the beginning.

Somewhere in time, there was a beginning. Well, a beginning as we see it. Our finite minds cannot comprehend the timeline of God. He has always been and always will be. Our minds have a hard time with that. We like to see things from a starting point. So, for the sake of our feeble minds, let's have a beginning. John 1:1-3 points out the beginning and who was there and what was accomplished.

*In the beginning was the Word, and the
Word was with God, and the Word was
God. He was in the beginning with God. All
things were made through Him, and without
Him nothing was made that was made.*

John points out that at the very beginning of things we find God and Christ. Then through Him, all things were made. The keyword here is "all" things. We know from Genesis 1:1 that *"In the beginning, God created the heavens and the earth."* But what about the things in heaven and on earth? The "all" that John spoke of is elaborated on in a letter Paul wrote to the Colossians. Paul says in Colossians 1:16:

*For by Him, all things were created that are
in heaven and that are on earth, visible and
invisible, whether thrones or dominions or
principalities or powers. All things were created through Him and for Him.*

From Paul's letter, we see that God created "all" things. Even the things that we know little or nothing about. He created the things in heaven and the things on the earth. Just to continue this thought for a second on creation, let's look at Psalm 148:1-5.

*Praise the LORD! Praise the LORD from
the heavens; Praise Him in the heights!
Praise Him, all His angels; Praise Him, all
His hosts! Praise Him, sun and moon; Praise
Him, all you stars of light! Praise Him, you*

heavens of heavens, And you waters above
the heavens! Let them praise the name of the
LORD, For He commanded and they were
created.

From this, we see with little doubt that God simply commanded, and "all" things were created. One of those commands was the creation of angels. He simply spoke, and they existed.

The angels themselves declare that they are creations of the Almighty. In Revelation 4:11 we find them proclaiming,

You are worthy, O Lord, To receive glory
and honor and power; For You created all
things, And by Your will they exist and were
created.

Not only do they proclaim the Lord as their creator, but they also give Him credit for their continued existence.

So then, angels were created by God just like you and me. However, when we read the story of creation in Genesis, we read nothing of the creation of angels. So, when were they created? We do not know the exact timing of the creation of angels nor is that important. Had the Lord wanted us to know that He would have told us. What we do know is that they were around to see God's handy work in the creation of our world and all that is in it.

One of my favorite parts of the Bible is near the end of the book of Job. In these last chapters of Job, we are reminded, as Job was, of the awesomeness of God. Job has had a bit of a rough time and has done his share of complaining to God. In this last part of Job, God tells him to stand up and be questioned. I don't know about you, but that would get my attention.

In chapter 38, God reveals His omnipotence to Job. Let's look specifically at verses 4-7 where God asks Job a series of questions.

> *Where were you when I laid the foundations of the earth? Tell Me, if you have understanding. Who determined its measurements? Surely you know! Or who stretched the line upon it? To what were its foundations fastened? Or who laid its cornerstone, When the morning stars sang together, And all the sons of God shouted for joy?*

Pay attention to that last part; *When the morning stars sang together, And all the sons of God shouted for joy?* Angels are not mentioned in the creation story of Genesis because they had already been created.

One of the functions of angels is to worship God, so they may have been around for millions of years before God created mankind. Then again, according to Hebrews 1:14, another function of angels is to be *"ministering spirits sent to serve those who will inherit salvation."* So, they may have been created just before mankind. Either way, the presence of Satan, formerly known as Lucifer, in the Garden of Eden in his already fallen state during the early chapters of our history back up what we find in Job. All leave little doubt that angels preceded us in creation where they had the magnificent pleasure of watching God create our entire universe. *"And all the sons of God shouted for joy."* How's that for a beginning?

CHAPTER THREE

SPIRITS

In the last chapter, we discussed the fact that angels are created beings. They were created by God just like you and me. Just like all our world, God simply spoke, and they came into existence. We don't know when that happened. We just know that it happened before our universe was created. Just like you, me, the animals, the Earth, and the stars, God created angels as well. We just saw from the previous scripture that God created all things. That "all" includes angels. We also saw how the angels themselves declare that they are a creation of God, but simply knowing that they are created beings doesn't tell us much about them. What we want to know is what they are.

Before we get into what angels are, allow me to stand on my soapbox and get straight to the point and clarify one important issue about angels and what they are not. They are not formerly humans, nor did they evolve from something else. Many times, I have heard it said following the loss of a loved one phrases like "so-and-so earned his angel wings today" or "Heaven gained another angel today." Let me be clear on this. When you die, you do not become an angel, nor will you ever be an angel. Humans and angels are separate creations of God. One never becomes the other.

I understand that this may give comfort to some after the loss of a loved one, but our comfort should come from knowing that our loved one, redeemed by the blood of the Lamb, is now standing before God, surrounded by angels, not becoming one of them. It is as simple as this; the Bible says many things about heaven and angels. Never does it say that we will become one.

Now that that is out of the way, let's get back to the question at hand. What are angels? Hebrews 1:14 refers to angels as *"ministering spirits"*. Unlike we humans, angels are spirit beings. What exactly is a spirit being?

A spirit being, an angel, does not occupy space and time in a material way like you and me. They have no weight, no size, and no reliance on time. The Bible uses some colorful imagery to demonstrate this aspect of angels. In Psalms 104 we find.

Who makes His angels spirits, His ministers a flame of fire.

And in Psalm 18,

And He rode upon a cherub and flew; He flew upon the wings of the wind.

David likened the angels to wind and fire. Wind and fire both are good examples of the spiritual world in that you can feel their effects but can hold neither. You can feel the wind blowing against your skin and the heat of the fire warming you. You can see the effects of both on our environment, but you cannot physically grab onto either of them or hold them in your hand. So, it is with angels. Yet, they are true beings and are as real as anything else in God's creation. Angels have personality, intelligence, emotions, and free will as we shall discuss shortly. We, humans, are in essence spiritual beings; however, by God's design, our existence requires four dimensions. Angels have no such requirement.

The physics of our world requires that we humans exist in three dimensions of space and one dimension of time. Well, sort of... I say "sort of" because according to some theoretical physicists who subscribe to String Theory, we exist in at least 10 dimensions of space and one of time. But for our discussion, let's keep it simple and just talk about the simple physics of the four dimensions.

To define where we are or where an object is in space, we use a coordinate system that allows for going forward and backward, left and right, and up and down. The x, y, and z-axis if you would. This allows us to pinpoint an exact location of an object. It would be like defining the location of an airplane at a particular moment of its flight. I could do so by its longitude, latitude, and altitude. Throw in time and we have, according to physics, the airplane's exact position in space and time. This is the framework God created for us to function.

That is how God designed our world and how our minds comprehend it. However, God did not put that limitation on angels. Because they are spirit beings without the limitations of our coordinate system, they are free to move about through space and time in ways that you and I will never comprehend this side of heaven. For instance, could it be possible for multiple dimensions of space and time to operate side-by-side? Dimensions that we cannot see or know of, yet they are there? Anything is possible with God. However, because we were created to operate in our four dimensions, we find it hard to grasp this concept and the possibility of its reality. This is one reason so many people have a hard time with the existence of heaven. Because heaven, at least initially, will be a spiritual place and outside the bounds of our simple physics, we have a hard time believing in or comprehending its existence. Let's look at an example from scripture of how the spiritual world exists side by side with our world without us even knowing it.

In 2 Kings 6, we find the Syrians at war with Israel. The king of Syria was moving across the country in hopes of ambushing the Israelites and the king of Israel in particular. But it seems that no matter where he went, the Israelites never passed that way. The king became suspicious that there was a spy in his ranks and called in his counsel to ask them about it. They informed him that there indeed was a spy, but it was not from inside the king's military ranks. It was Elisha, God's prophet. God was allowing Elisha to know every move that the Syrian king made so that he could warn the king of Israel of places to avoid. This infuriated the Syrian king. He wanted to take Elisha out of the picture so he inquired about where he could find him. His counsel informed him that Elisha was in Dothan. Immediately, the king sent a great army of horses and chariots to Dothan to capture or kill Elisha. Verse 14 picks up the story from there.

> Therefore, he sent horses and chariots and a great army there, and they came by night and surrounded the city. And when the servant of the man of God arose early and went out, there was an army, surrounding the city with horses and chariots. And his servant said to him, "Alas, my master! What shall we do?" So, he answered, "Do not fear, for those who are with us are more than those who are with

them." And Elisha prayed, and said, "LORD,
I pray, open his eyes that he may see." Then
the LORD opened the eyes of the young man,
and he saw. And behold, the mountain was
full of horses and chariots of fire all around
Elisha.

2 Kings 6:14-17

At this specific time in history, chariots and horses were formidable weapons. It would be like tanks and heavy artillery today. The Syrian king had sent out the big guns against Elisha. When Gehazi awoke and stepped out of the tent to begin his daily chores, he must have been awestruck to see that their camp was surrounded by hundreds if not thousands of soldiers along with the horses and chariots. Filled with fear, he ran back inside the tent to tell Elisha the bad news. Gehazi must have been amazed at how calm Elisha was about the situation. I could just hear Gehazi now, "no, you must not have heard me. There is an entire army with big guns surrounding our camp. We are done." I like what Elisha told Gehazi, *"for those who are with us are more than those who are with them."* With that, Elisha prayed that God would allow Gehazi to have the supernatural ability to see into that other dimension, the angelic dimension. When Gehazi's eyes were opened, he saw an amazing sight. Surrounding his camp was the Syrian army with all its horses and chariots. But surrounding them, was an army of angels. The angels did not just surround the Syrian army, the Bible says that the entire mountain was filled with horses and chariots of fire.

Just because we cannot see something does not mean that it is not there. You cannot see electricity but touch the end of a plug as you insert it into an electrical outlet, and you know that it is there. So, it is with angels. Just because they are not confined to our physical universe does not mean that they are not with us. As spirit beings, angels can be with us even when we do not know that they are here. God allowed Elisha and Gehazi to see this firsthand.

Since angels are "ministering spirits" perhaps they are not confined to space and time like we are so that they can be with us and minister to us without interfering in our lives. Think about it for a second; angels do the work of our Lord. We trust the Lord to meet our needs, watch over us, and protect us in every situation. I'm sure at times, He uses His angels to do that. If you could see that it was the angels assisting you, would your faith be in the Lord or the angels?

CHAPTER FOUR

WHAT DO ANGELS LOOK LIKE?

One of the most often asked questions about angels has to do with their appearance. What do angels look like? That is a hard question to answer since they are spiritual beings and in their natural state do not have any material form or shape. If they are spirits, could I see them anyway? Ask yourself, what does your spirit look like? We as humans have both a physical and spiritual side that make up who we are. Have you ever wondered what that spirit side is?

Perhaps, it is the part of you that does your thinking and feels emotion. Your body, the physical part of you, takes care of interacting with the world around you through your five senses. You can see, touch, smell, hear, and taste the world around you. But your emotions and thoughts cannot be touched or held physically, thus they are spiritual. These thoughts and emotions are just as much a part of who you are as your face or hands.

When talking about heaven being a spiritual place, people often wonder how they will be able to see and interact without a body. This is a natural question since our bodies are such an integral part of us and what we have used to interact with the world for all our lives. So, when we talk of interaction without a body, that brings us back to the question of what your spirit is. Perhaps the answer is as close as your next nap.

Just as we mentioned before, our five senses help us interact with the natural world. One of those senses is that of sight. Light bounces off the object you are looking at and comes into your eye through the cornea. The cornea helps to direct the light through the little dark circle in the center of your eye known as the pupil. The pupil, the opening in your eye that allows light through, opens or contracts by way of the iris. The iris is the colored part of your eye. They work in conjunction to control the amount of light entering your eye. The light then makes its way to the rear of your eye where cones and rods on the eye's retina are stimulated. These cones and rods then translate the visual information they are receiving into electrical information that is transferred to the brain via the optic nerve. The optic nerve is made up of tiny cells that relay the electric form of what you are seeing to the occipital cortex. Here the brain produces a visual map of the information, and your brain "sees" what your eyes are looking at.

"Seeing", as we know it, hinges on the fact that light is reflecting off some object and entering our eyes. But what about when our eyes are closed? What about when we are asleep? We all dream. Some of us pay little attention to it and yet others dream in technicolor where the dreams seem ultra-real. I am one of the latter. Most of my dreams seem very real to me and often contain lots of vivid details that, most often, I cannot explain. Now I am no dream expert, but I do realize that my dreams are products of my mind and emotions. Both of which make up parts of my spirit. So, perhaps "seeing" in a spiritual way is like dreaming. While dreaming, we "see" and interact with people and things around us without the aid of the five senses. In essence, what we are experiencing is solely through our spirit. Perhaps this is one reason we often see examples in the Bible of angels bringing messages to humans through dreams and visions. One spirit communicates with another. Now, I am not saying that what you experience through your dreams is any reflection of you spiritually. I simply make the example to point out that the spirit world can and does operate without the aid of our five senses. This brings us back around to our first question. If angels are spirits, what do they look like? In our limited human state of needing our five senses to describe what something looks like, we cannot answer that question.

Fortunately for us, our Lord knows all there is to know about us and is fully aware of our limitations of space and time. So, He made the angels in such a way that they could enter our world and interact with us. Sometimes this is through dreams and other times He allows them to take on the form of humans. The Bible warns us in Hebrews 13:2:

Do not forget to entertain strangers, for by so doing some have unwittingly entertained angels.

Most often when angels appeared to humans in the Bible, they looked like normal human men. In Genesis 18:1-19 we find:

Then the LORD appeared to him by the terebinth trees of Mamre, as he was sitting in the tent door in the heat of the day. So he lifted his eyes and looked, and behold, three men were standing by him; and when he saw them, he ran from the tent door to meet them, and bowed himself to the ground, and said,

"My Lord, if I have now found favor in Your sight, do not pass on by Your servant. Please let a little water be brought, wash your feet, and rest yourselves under the tree. And I will bring a morsel of bread, that you may refresh your hearts. After that, you may pass by, since you have come to your servant."

Two of these men were angels which we will talk more about later. The third was the Lord. Abraham saw these angels as men. He probably saw them dressed as any man in his day would have been dressed. But there was something different about them that allowed him to know that it was the Lord and two angels.

And in Joshua 5:13-15:

And it came to pass, when Joshua was by Jericho, that he lifted his eyes and looked, and behold, a Man stood opposite him with His sword drawn in His hand. And Joshua went to Him and said to Him, "Are You for us or for our adversaries?" So He said, "No, but as Commander of the army of the LORD I have now come." And Joshua fell on his face to the earth and worshiped, and said to Him, "What does my Lord say to His servant?" Then the Commander of the LORD's army said to Joshua, "Take your sandal off your foot, for the place where you stand is holy." And Joshua did so.

And then in Luke 24:1-8;

> *Now on the first day of the week, very early*
> *in the morning, they, and certain other*
> *women with them, came to the tomb bring-*
> *ing the spices which they had prepared. But*
> *they found the stone rolled away from the*
> *tomb. Then they went in and did not find*
> *the body of the Lord Jesus. And it happened,*
> *as they were greatly perplexed about this,*
> *that behold, two men stood by them in shin-*
> *ing garments. Then, as they were afraid*
> *and bowed their faces to the earth, they*
> *said to them, "Why do you seek the living*
> *among the dead? He is not here but is risen!*
> *Remember how He spoke to you when He*
> *was still in Galilee, saying, 'The Son of Man*
> *must be delivered into the hands of sinful*
> *men, and be crucified, and the third day rise*
> *again.'" And they remembered His words.*

Other times in the Bible we see angels appearing to humans not as men but as something unworldly. Something not ordinarily seen by the human eye. For example, Ezekiel chapter 1 describes the cherubim, a type of angel, like this.

> *Now it came to pass in the thirtieth year, in the*
> *fourth month, on the fifth day of the month, as*
> *I was among the captives by the River Chebar,*
> *that the heavens were opened and I saw visions*
> *of God. On the fifth day of the month, which was*
> *in the fifth year of King Jehoiachin's captivity,*

the word of the LORD came expressly to Eze-
kiel the priest, the son of Buzi, in the land of the
Chaldeans by the River Chebar; and the hand of
the LORD was upon him there.
Then I looked, and behold, a whirlwind was
coming out of the north, a great cloud with
raging fire engulfing itself; and brightness was
all around it and radiating out of its midst like
the color of amber, out of the midst of the fire.
Also from within it came the likeness of four
living creatures. And this was their appearance:
they had the likeness of a man. Each one had
four faces, and each one had four wings. Their
legs were straight, and the soles of their feet were
like the soles of calves' feet. They sparkled like
the color of burnished bronze. The hands of a
man were under their wings on their four sides;
and each of the four had faces and wings. Their
wings touched one another. The creatures did not
turn when they went, but each one went straight
forward.
As for the likeness of their faces, each had the
face of a man; each of the four had the face of a
lion on the right side, each of the four had the
face of an ox on the left side, and each of the four
had the face of an eagle. Thus were their faces.
Their wings stretched upward; two wings of each
one touched one another, and two covered their
bodies. And each one went straight forward; they
went wherever the spirit wanted to go, and they
did not turn when they went.
As for the likeness of the living creatures, their
appearance was like burning coals of fire, like
the appearance of torches going back and forth
among the living creatures. The fire was bright,

*and out of the fire went lightning. And the living
creatures ran back and forth, in appearance like a
flash of lightning.*

*Now as I looked at the living creatures, behold, a
wheel was on the earth beside each living creature with its four faces. The appearance of the
wheels and their workings was like the color of
beryl, and all four had the same likeness. The
appearance of their workings was, as it were,
a wheel in the middle of a wheel. When they
moved, they went toward any one of four directions; they did not turn aside when they went.
As for their rims, they were so high they were
awesome; and their rims were full of eyes, all
around the four of them. When the living creatures went, the wheels went beside them; and
when the living creatures were lifted up from the
earth, the wheels were lifted up. Wherever the
spirit wanted to go, they went, because there the
spirit went; and the wheels were lifted together
with them, for the spirit of the living creatures
was in the wheels. When those went, these went;
when those stood, these stood; and when those
were lifted up from the earth, the wheels were
lifted up together with them, for the spirit of the
living creatures was in the wheels.*

*The likeness of the firmament above the heads
of the living creatures was like the color of an
awesome crystal, stretched out over their heads.
And under the firmament their wings spread out
straight, one toward another. Each one had two
which covered one side, and each one had two
which covered the other side of the body. When
they went, I heard the noise of their wings, like
the noise of many waters, like the voice of the*

Almighty, a tumult like the noise of an army; and
when they stood still, they let down their wings.
A voice came from above the firmament that was
over their heads; whenever they stood, they let
down their wings.

Ezekiel 1:1-25

Whenever angels appeared to people in the Bible it was
either hard for them to describe, or so incredible that it was
terrifying because the people seemed to always be afraid.
This is evident because the first words spoken by the angels
were often *"do not be afraid."* Luke even goes so far as to say
that the shepherds in the fields the night Jesus was born
were *"sore afraid"* when the angels appeared to them. Sometimes angels appear to have wings and at other times they
appear to have human and animal characteristics such as
faces and feet. They apparently speak our language and
can be heard praising God. And in fact, by the example
of the angels coming with the Lord to see Abraham, they
could also eat. I could just imagine that private conversation
between the Lord and the angels; "Do they really eat this
stuff every day?" or "I told you it was different."

So, to answer the question of what angels look like is
rather complicated. But one thing is for certain, God knows
how we perceive our world and presents the angels to us in
whatever form is necessary to accomplish His will. As we
progress through the remaining chapters, this will become
evident. But for now, let's look at some basics.

Male or Female

First off, are angels male or female? Throughout the Bible, every reference to angels is in the masculine gender. The Greek word for angel in the New Testament, *angelos*, is in the masculine form. There is no feminine form of the word *angelos*. All references to names for angels in the Bible are masculine. Michael, Gabriel, Lucifer - all are names for men. Whenever the Bible speaks of angels, it always uses masculine grammar. For instance, in Luke 1:29 *"Mary was troubled at his (Gabriel's) words."* Isaiah 14:12 speaking of Satan says *"Oh, Lucifer, son of the morning."* And yet again in Judges 6:21, the angel holds a staff in *his* hand. And on and on. In addition, whenever an angel appeared in human form it was dressed in men's clothing. No angel ever appears in the Bible dressed as a woman.

Some refer to Zechariah 5:9 as an example of female angels. Zechariah 5:9 reads:

> *Then I raised my eyes and looked, and there*
> *were two women, coming with the wind*
> *in their wings; for they had wings like the*
> *wings of a stork, and they lifted up the basket*
> *between earth and heaven.*

To some, the fact that they had wings depicts them as angels. The problem with this lies in the fact that the women in this prophetic vision are not called angels, but are called *nashiym*. The same word used for the woman in the basket in the preceding verses, 7 and 8, represents wickedness. The angel that Zechariah was speaking to was called a *malak*. *Malak* is a completely different word that is from the Old Testament Hebrew which meant messenger or angel. So, the argument that these were female angels does not stand.

Some people feel that angels are genderless. They formulate this idea from Matthew 22:30 which reads.

> *For in the resurrection they neither marry*
> *nor are given in marriage, but are like angels*
> *of God in heaven.*

The purpose behind gender and marriage is procreation. Some feel that because the verse says that we will be like the angels and neither marry nor be given in marriage that the angels are genderless. After all, if there is no procreation, then there is no need for gender. The fact that there is no marriage or procreation has nothing to do with having gender. But given today's society with those that are confused about gender....well, you see where I am going with this.

We must not confuse gender in our language with the fact that angels might be male or female as we know it. Remember two important points here. Angels are completely separate beings from you and me. Who are we to try and assign gender to beings we know little about? Further, for us to assign gender other than the masculine would be inappropriate, and here is why. The masculine gender pronouns in our language often refer to authority more than to a particular sex. God always refers to Himself in the masculine. He has complete authority over us. Scripture makes it clear that angels are of a higher order than humans and have certain authorities that have been granted by God to them. Simply look at 2 Kings 19:35 and Luke 2:10. Angels wield His power, carry His messages, and represent Him on earth. So, it would be inappropriate for us to disregard this hierarchy and refer to them as anything other than masculine.

Before I move on, I would like to leave you with another interesting point that you might find fascinating. As we have found, the Bible never mentions anything about an angel being female. It's curious to note, that it never refers to them as children either; only adult males. Something to think about the next time you see a little figurine depicting an angel as a child.

Wings

When we see an artist's rendition of an angel, it almost always has wings and maybe a halo. It is probably dressed in a white robe with blonde hair and quite possibly playing the harp - but it has wings. We even see it as a little naked chubby baby with wings. What is it with the wings?

Most of the angels that appear to humans in the Bible do so in the human form. Not humans with wings, but simply humans. Whether these angels have wings in their natural state is unclear. Remember, angels are spirit beings with no particular shape or mass as we know it. Furthermore, why would a spirit need wings? Since they are not limited by the physical laws of our universe, they would not need wings as a mode of transportation. However, it is still possible for them to have wings.

There are two types of angels that we do know have wings, the cherubim, and seraphim. We will look at both angels in detail in another chapter, but for now, it is enough to know that some angels do indeed have wings.

In my mother's house are many little figurines of angels. They all have wings. Paintings and illustrations of angels all depict them with wings. This is how we have come to know angels. We have formulated this image for angels in our attempt to know them and to distinguish them from normal human forms. Giving them wings helps us to recognize them in images and establishes a needed sense of order. After all, since we have already determined that it is next to impossible for us as humans to describe what a spirit looks like, it would be awfully hard to paint a picture of one. There is nothing wrong with imagining angels with wings because some do have wings. The important thing is for us to realize that angels can take on any form God desires to accomplish His will - wings or no wings.

CHAPTER FIVE

EMOTIONS, INTELLIGENCE, AND WILL

As of 2019, approximately 7.6 billion people were living on our planet. Over 328 million of those were right here in the United States. It is interesting to think that biologically, none of those 7.6 billion people are alike. God made each one unique. Each is unique in their height and weight, the color of their eyes, hair, and skin; all are unique right down to the very DNA that makes up who they are. Each one has a unique personality.

The Bible tells us that God, with the angels looking on, made us in His image. Genesis 1:26 says.

> *Then God said, "Let Us make man in Our image according to Our likeness.*

We were made in the image of God. God created us with our unique bodies and within those bodies, he placed unique personalities. He created each one with a *"likeness"* of God Himself.

Thinking along those lines raises the following question. If we were made with these unique personalities, do angels have them as well, or do they at least share in some of the same traits that make up our personalities?

Scholars say that our personalities are made up of three important elements. Those elements are emotion, intelligence, and will. If these three elements can be found in the lives of angels, then it follows that they too have unique personalities of their own.

When it comes to the matter of emotions, intelligence, and will in angels, one must remember that angels are a higher order of creation than humans. Therefore, it would stand as a basic assumption that their emotions, intelligence, and will would also be of a higher order than ours. How much higher will remain a mystery until we find ourselves among them in Heaven. For now, we must be satisfied simply to answer the question of do they indeed possess these characteristics. For that, we turn to the only source we have on the subject, the Bible.

Emotions

Let's start with emotions. Some feel that our emotions are what truly make us human. They are what bind us together as family, friends, and sometimes enemies. The word emotion means an instinctive state of mind that comes from one's circumstances, mood, or relationship with other people. We are happy, sad, angry, or excited depending on our circumstances. The funny thing about our emotions is that we usually cannot control them. We may not outwardly show what we are feeling, but we feel the way we do, nonetheless. The Bible gives several examples of angels having these same emotions.

One emotion that we often experience is fear. In James 2:19 we find.

You believe that there is one God. You do
well. Even the demons believe-and tremble!

Demons are nothing more than fallen angels. This verse makes it clear that they tremble in fear. As they should. They have much to fear. They may not fear the same things that we humans do; but, when it comes to Jesus, they are horrified. This is evidence that they positively possess the emotion of fear just as you and I do.

Along with fear comes anger. We know that Satan is a fallen angel and therefore representative of other angels. In Revelation, we find John describing Satan during the end times being enraged. Revelation 12:17 says:

And the dragon was enraged with the
woman, and he went to make war with the
rest of her offspring, who keep the command-
ments of God and have the testimony of Jesus
Christ.

As evil as Satan is, I can only imagine the amount of anger he can generate. This anger is surely carried over to his demons as well. All of which is evident in the evil that is so perverse in our world today. As horrible as this anger and perversion are, the Bible tells us that it only gets worse during the end times. Satan and his demons are simply fallen angels. Therefore, this demonstrates that angels do possess the two basic emotions of fear and anger.

The opposite of fear and anger is joy and happiness. Jesus says Himself that angels feel joy. In Luke 15:10 He tells us.

> *Likewise, I say to you, there is joy in the presence of the angels of God over one sinner who repents.*

The angels do not know what it is like to experience salvation and redemption because they have never needed them. However, they certainly understand what it means for a human to receive the gift of salvation and eternal life. They have always been in the presence of God and know firsthand what is in store for us when we step into eternity. In addition, they were there when God formed His creation and even rejoiced. So, it is understandable that they would experience joy in the fact that a part of that creation has been redeemed and is destined to share in their experience of being with the Lord for all eternity.

As mentioned above, the angels experienced joy during the creation of the universe. Job 38:7 tells us that at the creation, the angels shouted with joy.

> *When the morning stars sang together, And all the sons of God shouted for joy?*

Just imagine what that must have been like, watching God form creation out of nothing. Watching Him turn a black void into a colorful masterpiece. The Bible says that He simply spoke, and it came into being; that He simply breathed creation into existance. Just think about that for a second. What a magnificent sight that must have been. I can fully understand why the angels shouted for joy.

One of the things that we humans take joy in is humor. We all like a good joke and often laugh at things in life that we find amusing. Angels share this characteristic. In Numbers 22, we find the Angel of the Lord interrupting Balaam's journey. He could have simply shown himself and stopped him or caused the donkey Balaam was riding to simply die. But instead, He caused the donkey to turn its course several times. In so doing, Balaam whipped the donkey. What follows is a demonstration of emotion through humor. The angel of the Lord caused the donkey to speak. Here we have a man carrying on a conversation with a sarcastic donkey. Now that's funny.

What about some of our more serious emotions? Angels must certainly share in those as well. They do, and we as Christians would do well to learn from them. Take for instance the emotions of reverence and loyalty.

Often in our hurried lives, we tend to forget who it is that we are praying to. We sometimes find ourselves rushing through our prayers, simply going through the motions. We lose faith, forgetting that we have an all-powerful Father. We tend to forget that the One that we pray to and put our trust in is the creator of the universe, the Lord God Almighty. Angels never lose sight of either of those things. They live in a constant state of awareness of that fact. We see a demonstration of this in Isaiah 6:3. Here we find Isaiah describing the Seraphim. Isaiah says:

And one cried to another and said: "Holy, holy, holy is the LORD of hosts; The whole earth is full of His glory!

Angels are in constant praise and reverence of God for who He is. They never lose sight of the fact that God is the creator and sustainer of all existence. We on the other hand, get so wrapped up in our lives that we either forget or take it for granted. For example, you are at the end of a long day and sit down for your evening meal. As is your habit; you bow your head, close your eyes, and begin to thank God for the food you are about to eat. How many times is that done to simply check the box, if you would, to fulfill the obligation because we know we are supposed to? How many times do we really meditate on who it is we are talking to and what it really means for God to have supplied the food we are about to eat? For most of us, we have way more on our tables than we need, and certainly tastier and more enjoyable food than most of the world. If we want to experience true prayer in our Christian walks, we must learn from the angels and come to Him in a true state of reverence. We must never forget that He not only supplies our needs, but most often gives us more than we deserve.

Loyalty is an emotion that we as humans demonstrate on occasion, depending on the circumstances. We are loyal to our friends and family for the most part and depending on the demands, to our nation and community as well. We like to say that we are loyal to God and the Word, but our sinful world hampers us at times from that commitment. Angels are not hampered by such things. Throughout the Bible, the one emotion that angels demonstrate the most is a complete sense of loyalty to God. This is demonstrated by their unquestioning obedience to Him. Angels never question, they simply obey. We humans almost always question. But angels have learned that God's wisdom is so great that any command He gives is worthy of obedience. It is out of loyalty and reverence for our very creator that they obey without question. We Christians would do well to emulate this trait of our angelic brothers.

Since we are on the topic of emotions, allow me to take a side track here for a moment and mention something that you might find fascinating. When God created us, He gifted us with a colorful array of characteristics. One of those characteristics is the ability to be creative. Some of us are more creative than others, but regardless, we all possess the innate need to create. No place is this more evident than in music. Whether it is music for a symphony orchestra or a simple child's song, music is created as a direct result of our emotions. We have happy music, sad music, music that inspires us, and music that reaches the full gamut of our emotions. All of us have that song that when heard makes us remember some good times in the past, and we smile because it makes us happy. Even though any of our emotions can be expressed through music, no other emotion brings a song to the heart like happiness and joy. Since the angels share in our emotions of happiness and joy, it would be natural for us to assume that these emotions also bring a song to their hearts as well. Surely they must sing. After all, who hasn't heard of the Angel Chorus? Didn't the angels sing to the shepherds when they appeared to them in the field that first Christmas morning? Aren't the angels around God's throne singing "Holy holy holy..."?

A good friend, and wise man, whom I hold in high regard, brought out an interesting point that I had never considered. A point that I had always simply took for granted. It may surprise you, as it did me, that the Bible gives almost no indication that angels sing. I use the word "almost" because most of the scripture that we traditionally think of when it comes to angels singing says "saying" not "singing". However, there are a few verses that may indicate that they do sing. Let me explain.

The event that most are likely to associate with angels singing is found in the Christmas story, when the angels appear to the shepherds in the field. For this story, we turn to Luke 2. Specifically, let's look at verses 8 – 14.

> *Now there were in the same country shepherds living out in the fields, keeping watch over their flock by night. And behold, an angel of the Lord stood before them, and the glory of the Lord shone around them, and they were greatly afraid. Then the angel said to them, "Do not be afraid, for behold, I bring you good tidings of great joy which will be to all people. For there is born to you this day in the city of David a Savior, who is Christ the Lord. And this will be the sign to you: You will find a Babe wrapped in swaddling cloths, lying in a manger."*
> *And suddenly there was with the angel a multitude of the heavenly host praising God and saying:*
> *"Glory to God in the highest,*
> *And on earth peace, goodwill toward men!"*

Most of us, when we hear this scripture imagine a multitude of angels singing in the sky while the shepherds look on in amazement from their fields. But notice what it says in verse 13. *"praising God and saying:"* The key word there is "saying". The thought of millions of angels in the sky singing praises to God over that beautiful pastureland of Israel would be an awesome sight to see. That's exactly what the shepherds saw…. except the angels weren't singing, the Bible says they were saying.

But alas you say, angels do sing. It says so in Job 38:7. Well, let's look. Job 38:7 says,

Where were you when I laid the foundations
of the earth?
Tell Me, if you have understanding.
Who determined its measurements?
Surely you know!
Or who stretched the line upon it?
To what were its foundations fastened?
Or who laid its cornerstone,
When the morning stars sang together,
And all the sons of God shouted for joy?

Job 38:4-7

Morning stars are widely believed to be angels. So right there in verse 7, it says that they *"sang together."* It does; however, the Hebrew word used for "sang" is "be-ran". If I am not mistaken, this is the only place in scripture where it is found. It sometimes means "sing" but primarily means "joyfully shouted", "resoundingly cried", or "rejoiced". Thus, the "almost" from above. They could have indeed been singing, but most likely, they were simply joyfully shouting. We just don't know for sure which one they were doing, but we do know they were truly happy about what was taking place.

Another verse that contributes to the "almost" from above is Revelation 5:9. In Revelation 5, we find Jesus taking the scroll that is sealed with the seven seals; the only one worthy to take the scroll. When Jesus takes the scroll, all of heaven praises Him. Let's look at this starting in verse 8.

Now when He had taken the scroll, the four
living creatures and the twenty-four elders
fell down before the Lamb, each having a
harp, and golden bowls full of incense, which
are the prayers of the saints. And they sang a
new song, saying:
"You are worthy to take the scroll,
And to open its seals;
For You were slain,
And have redeemed us to God by Your blood
Out of every tribe and tongue and people and
nation,
And have made us kings and priests to our
God;
And we shall reign on the earth."

Without going into detail, the twenty-four elders are not believed by scholars to be angels; however, the four living creatures are. If indeed they are angels, the Bible is clear in this instance they do indeed sing, *"and they sang a new song..."* Of course, they haven't sung that song yet, but will very shortly.

This topic could be debated by religious scholars to antiquity. Regardless of which side of the fence you stand on, Rev 5:9 clears up the question of whether angels sing or not. One must walk away from this knowing that singing by the angels, at least as far as the Bible indicates, is quite rare. I don't know about you, but learning that angels didn't sing changed my Christmas story.

Intelligence

What about intelligence? Having intelligence is not just about being smart. There are a lot of smart people with no common sense. Intelligence is the ability to acquire and apply knowledge. That's where wisdom comes from. Wisdom is being able to look at a circumstance and apply the knowledge one possesses to create the appropriate outcome. Therefore, one could say that if a person demonstrates wisdom, then they possess intelligence. But, how does one obtain wisdom? Wisdom is obtained by learning from our mistakes or the mistakes of others. It is also learned through the trial and error of application of the knowledge that we have. Angels have an advantage in this area. Since they are not limited in space and time as we are, they are able to not only learn from themselves, but can learn from observing us as well. For instance, in 1 Corinthians 4:9, we find:

For I think that God has displayed us, the apostles, last, as men condemned to death; for we have been made a spectacle to the world, both to angels and to men.

As we go about our daily lives, the angels are watching us. I am sure they are curious about many things that we do because a lot of what we do must seem strange to them. But one thing is clear from this verse, they observe and learn from the things that we do.

God also imparts His wisdom directly to them so they can accomplish the tasks He has created them for. We see Paul speaking of this in Ephesians 3:10-11.

> *to the intent that now the manifold wisdom*
> *of God might be made known by the church*
> *to the principalities and powers in the heav-*
> *enly places,*

Just as God imparted His grace on Paul giving him all that he needed to preach the Gospel of Jesus Christ, God imparts His wisdom to His angels so that they can do His work. Imagine the wisdom the angels must have to obey God's will, unquestioningly, in all circumstances. Oh, if only we humans had that wisdom.

Another characteristic of a person with intelligence is a certain level of curiosity. Intelligent people are always looking at the world around them and asking the question - why? Why does that happen? Why does that work? Why is that necessary? Let's look at 1 Peter 1:12.

> *To them it was revealed that, not to them-*
> *selves, but to us they were ministering the*
> *things which now have been reported to you*
> *through those who have preached the gospel*
> *to you by the Holy Spirit sent from heav-*
> *en-things which angels desire to look into.*

Peter had been speaking about our salvation and the faith we have through that salvation of the inheritance of heaven. Here we find a clear difference between angels and humans. Because angels are heavenly creatures who are in the presence of our Lord daily, they have never experienced life separate from Him. You and I have. Our sin separates us from the Almighty, and if it were not for the saving grace of our Lord through the sacrifice of His son, we would be eternally separated. Our salvation through Christ is unique to us. Angels have no need for it and have not experienced the emotions that go along with it. They do not need faith because they see the Lord daily. They watch firsthand His mighty omnipotence. We, on the other hand, must rely on our faith to help us hold our course until our life is complete and our salvation is brought into reality as we enter heaven and His presence. So, it stands to reason that this is something that the angels would be curious about and *"desire to look into."*

Will

Now that we have considered the fact that angels have emotions and demonstrate intelligence, let's look at whether angels can exercise those emotions and intelligence through free will. Will is defined as a person's choice or desire in a particular situation. You and I exercise our free will daily. It may be as complicated as how you will respond to circumstances, or as simple as whether to have that second piece of chocolate cake. Although, that choice can at times be very complicated, especially at a church social.

To see an example of angels exercising their will, we must look no further than Satan and his demons. We will talk more about them in a later chapter, but for now, let's look at it from the standpoint of an angel's ability to utilize his will. In Isaiah, we find the story of the fall of Lucifer. Looking at Isaiah 14:12-15 we find:

How you are fallen from heaven, O Lucifer, son of the morning! How you are cut down to the ground, You who weakened the nations! For you have said in your heart: 'I will ascend into heaven, I will exalt my throne above the stars of God; I will also sit on the mount of the congregation On the farthest sides of the north; I will ascend above the heights of the clouds, I will be like the Most High.' Yet you shall be brought down to Sheol, To the lowest depths of the Pit.

It is clear through Isaiah that Lucifer acted upon his will. As the rest of the story goes, he convinced a third of the angels in heaven to do the same thing; all making a conscious choice. All exercising their will in the choice they made to follow Lucifer.

So it is that angels have emotions, demonstrate intelligence, and exercise their will. Therefore, it is likely that each angel has his own unique personality just as we humans do. Just like us, there are probably funny angels and serious angels. As well as enjoying all that heaven has to offer, it will be a joy getting to know these heavenly creatures on a personal level.

In addition to their unique personalities, they also possess an incredible amount of knowledge about God, creation, life, and an infinite number of topics. They also seem to be incredibly strong, and always in the right place at the right time. As impressive as all of this sounds, angels do have their limitations

---

CHAPTER SIX

LIMITATIONS

When we look at illustrations and paintings of angels, it is easy to get the idea that they are superheroes. After all, they are often seen as these magnificent creatures with either perfect physiques wielding a sword and saving the day, or as beautiful winged beings there to do the impossible. The stories in the Bible also go a long way to build up their superhero status. These stories most often include them demonstrating incredible feats of strength and bravery. At other times, they seem to have supernatural powers of foresight and knowledge; all of which make up superheroes. When you stop and think about it, compared to us, they are superheroes. However, even Superman and all his super friends in the Halls of Justice could not pull off the things that Revelation says that the angels will do. Aside from Jesus, all superheroes have their limitations. Just as Superman had his limitations, so do the angels.

When God created man, He placed many limitations on us. I don't know if God gave angels an assortment of limitations like He did humans; but one thing is certain, there are three areas where angels are limited that we humans often misunderstand. It is these three areas that I would like to focus on in this chapter.

Angels are often misunderstood to be omnipresent, omniscient, and omnipotent; what I like to call the three "Omnis". Since these are the areas where many misunderstand the limitations of angels, let's look at each of these individually and see just how limited angels are.

Omnipresent

We have established the fact that angels are spiritual beings and as such are not limited by space and time. This allows them the ability to move about through creation in any way that God desires them to. They may be here one minute and there the next. However, having the ability to travel through space and time at will does not imply that they can be everywhere at once. The ability to be everywhere at the same time is known as being omnipresent. Only God is omnipresent. God has been, is now, and will be in an infinite number of places simultaneously. Most of us think of geographic locations when we think of God being in multiple places at the same time. However, He is also in multiple times simultaneously. He is anywhere on the time-line from the distant past to the distant future and everywhere inbetween. David talked about God's omnipresence in Psalm 139.

> *Where can I go from Your Spirit? Or where*
> *can I flee from Your presence? If I ascend*
> *into heaven, You are there; If I make my*
> *bed in hell, behold, You are there. If I take*
> *the wings of the morning, And dwell in the*

uttermost parts of the sea, Even there Your
hand shall lead me, And Your right hand
shall hold me. If I say, "Surely the darkness
shall fall on me," Even the night shall be light
about me; Indeed, the darkness shall not hide
from You, But the night shines as the day;
The darkness and the light are both alike to
You.

It is hard for us to wrap our minds around that. But, what a comfort to know that God will always be there. Just think about it for a minute; wherever you go or whatever you are going through, He is there. That big event in your life that is years down the road, He is already there. We never have to wait on or look for God, because He is perfectly on-time, everywhere at the same time. All the times in life when things aren't going as you would like and you wonder where God has gone; take heart because He has been, is now, and always will be right there by your side.

Angels, however, are only where the Lord dictates for them to be. I think that one reason we sometimes feel that angels are omnipresent is because they are perfectly where they need to be at just the right time. We need to remember, however, that this is not because of their own ability to be omnipresent, but because of God's unfailing faithfulness to watch over us.

Omniscient

One of the major characteristics of angels is their incredible knowledge. They have been in the presence of our Lord, watched over all creation, and have had a front-row seat watching mankind flail through life. But even with all of this, they are still not all-knowing. Being all-knowing is called being omniscient. Like being omnipresent, God is the only one who is omniscient. Jesus pointed this out in Matthew 24:36.

But of that day and hour no one knows, not
even the angels of heaven, but My Father
only.

Jesus was speaking of the end times and when the second coming would occur. He points out that not even the angels in heaven who are in God's presence daily know when that hour will occur. If they were omniscient, they would know, but they are not. Omniscience is reserved for God Himself. He knows all the stars by name, every hair on your head, and every trouble that you experience. Just think about that for a second. There are over 7 billion people on the planet, and He knows every detail about them from the hair on their heads, to the smallest parts that make up their biological structure. His knowledge is not limited to us but to every aspect of our universe right down to the nuclear reactions going on in stars that we cannot even see. Angels may be able to travel to every corner of our universe, but they cannot claim to know everything about it.

I once heard it said that you cannot surprise God with a joke because He already knows the punch line. I have often thought about that and somehow that brings me comfort. As I have dealt with circumstances in my life, it has brought me much comfort to know that God already knows the outcome of those circumstances. Not only that, but He also promises in His word that those circumstances will work *"to the good for those who love the Lord."*, Romans 8:28.

Combine omniscient and omnipresence, and He not only knows what you're going through and what you need, He is already there for you as well. In fact, in some ways, one could argue that the problem has long since been solved since God is as far in the future as He is in the past or present.

Omnipotent

This brings us around to the third of the "Omni's", omnipotence. Omnipotent means being all-powerful. As powerful as angels appear to be, they are limited in what they can do. In Daniel chapter 10, the Bible tells of an angel being detained by the powers of the demonic world. This angel eventually had to have the help of Michael the arch-angel. If angels were omnipotent, the angel would have needed no such help. Like omnipresent and omniscient, only God is omnipotent. God endows His creation with the power necessary to perform the tasks for which they were created. Although angels can be quite powerful beings, they are not omnipotent.

Look at Revelation 5 for instance.

> *And I saw in the right hand of Him who sat*
> *on the throne a scroll written inside and on*
> *the back, sealed with seven seals. Then I saw*
> *a strong angel proclaiming with a loud voice,*
> *"Who is worthy to open the scroll and to*
> *loose its seals?" And no one in heaven or on*

the earth or under the earth was able to open
the scroll, or to look at it.

As mighty as some of the angels are, none of them were worthy or powerful enough to open the scrolls. Notice that the scripture even says that it was a "strong" angel who was asking the question. Only Jesus was worthy and powerful enough to open the scrolls.

Hollywood and our own imaginations have gone a long way in giving angels the image of being all powerful. However, there is a big difference between being supernaturally strong and being all powerful.

In our hurried lives where we tend to want to deal with things on our terms and in our time, we forget that we have a God that is all powerful. Since He created everything in Heaven and on Earth, it only makes sense that He is more powerful than anything in either, and that includes angels.

Considering all the above, it is clear that angels have their limitations. The three omnis we have mentioned are reserved for the Lord Almighty Himself. He is omnipresent, omniscient, and omnipotent. Combined, He knows where you are in life and what you are going through, and is already there to comfort and strengthen you. He is there with His unlimited power and resources to help you. Most of all, He is there with His unlimited, unfailing, and unconditional love - just for you. Oh, angels are there to minister to you as well; but, they are there at the command of our Lord.

There is no doubt that angels have supernatural abilities to appear anywhere, at any time, and in any circumstance. There is also no doubt that they have been endowed with tremendous knowledge and strength. But we must be careful not to give them credit for characteristics that are reserved for God Himself.

Immortality

Before we leave this topic of limitations, there is one very important aspect of angels that we should cover. This aspect is that of immortality. We humans, are limited due to the curse of sin. Death is a byproduct of the very thing that separates us from God. When God created Adam and Eve and placed them in the garden, He did so with the plan that they would live and fellowship with Him forever. Sin changed all of that. If you look at the lifespan of man as the Old Testament progresses, you find that it gets shorter and shorter finally settling down around 70 years or so. The average life expectancy for the period of 2010-2015 was 71.1 years. Now whether this is due to the level of sin itself or because the earth was being populated and the Lord in His infinite wisdom decided that man did not need to live that long is beyond our knowing. Either way, on average we live around 70-80 years. Not so with the angels; as limited as they are in other areas, they are not limited by death. They are immortal. The angels that surround God and tend to His business in the heavenly realm are not subject to sin like you and me. Death has never entered their world. The same angels that watched as God created our world are the same angels that exist today and will be the same angels that we see in Heaven. Jesus was talking with the Sadducees about the resurrection in Luke 20. In that discussion, He makes this statement in verse 36.

nor can they die anymore, for they are equal
to the angels and are sons of God, being sons
of the resurrection.

Jesus was trying to get them to comprehend the resurrection and in so doing compares the resurrected to the angels in that they will become immortal. Jesus' death on the cross defeated sin and removed the barrier that would forever separate us from God. Doing so, paved the way for our immortality in the heavenly realm where we will be given that precious gift the angels already possess. That is the gift of eternally being in the presence of our Lord.

PART TWO

ANGELS OF THE BIBLE

CHAPTER SEVEN

CHERUBIM

*So He drove out the man; and He placed
cherubim at the east of the garden of Eden,
and a flaming sword which turned every
way, to guard the way to the tree of life.*

Genesis 3:24

Can you imagine what it must have been like? Adam and Eve lived in the most beautiful place that ever existed. The sky must have been crystal blue, never having been polluted by man or time. The vegetation was surely lush, green, and full of beautiful flowers of all sizes, shapes, and colors. Animals wandered about in perfect harmony with one another, never threatening each other or the two humans that lived there. The garden must have been such a beautifully perfect place that our minds cannot even begin to imagine its true splendor. A perfect place never tarnished until that one fateful day when sin entered the heart of man. Because of sin, God could no longer allow Adam and Eve to be residents of such a wonderful place that was home to things such as the tree of life.

One day they are walking with God in the awe-inspiring garden, and the next they are being driven out into the wilderness to *"till the ground from which he was taken."* What must have been going through their minds as they walked, or possibly ran out of the garden through what was no doubt a magnificent gate? They probably felt fear for the first time as they surely noticed the change in the land, the vegetation, the air, the light, and every other aspect of their environment as they left the only home humans had ever known. As they moved farther from the gate, I can imagine them turning to see that not only was the mighty gate closed, but it was guarded by an amazing group of angels guarding the way to the tree of life. These angels, Genesis 3:24 tells us, were Cherubim.

The Hebrew root word for Cherub is "kruwb" – pronounced ker-oob. It is an interesting word that occurs ninety-one times in the King James Version of the Bible, sixty-four times as the word Cherubim, and twenty-seven times as Cherub. Although angels are talked about throughout, the Cherubim are by far the most frequently mentioned heavenly creatures in the Hebrew Bible. Because of this, we can deduce that they must hold a special place with God our Father. Some would argue that the Cherubim are at the top of the angelic hierarchy.

Angels at the top of the angelic hierarchy are no doubt some of the most beautiful, yet powerful of all the heavenly hosts. Ezekiel tells us that Satan himself was a Cherub before he was kicked out of heaven. In Ezekiel 28:12-15 we find.

> *Son of man, take up a lamentation for the*
> *king of Tyre, and say to him, 'Thus says the*
> *Lord GOD: "You were the seal of perfection,*
> *Full of wisdom and perfect in beauty. You*

were in Eden, the garden of God; Every precious stone was your covering: The sardius, topaz, and diamond, Beryl, onyx, and jasper, Sapphire, turquoise, and emerald with gold. The workmanship of your timbrels and pipes Was prepared for you on the day you were created. "You were the anointed cherub who covers; I established you; You were on the holy mountain of God; You walked back and forth in the midst of fiery stones. You were perfect in your ways from the day you were created, till iniquity was found in you."

Through this scripture, we can see that as a Cherub, Satan was described as *"a seal of perfection, full of wisdom and perfect in beauty."* This leaves little doubt that the Cherubs are some of the most beautiful creatures in all of creation. Along with their beauty comes the power and wisdom that only the Lord can bestow. After all, there is no doubt that Satan is powerful, and he was a cherub. The image of the Cherubim guarding the gate leading to the Garden of Eden and the Tree of Life conjures up thoughts of powerful warriors ready for battle. We see through the eyes of Ezekiel that when talking about the cherubim, we are talking about a very beautiful and elite group of angels.

In the Bible, we find this elite order of angels as guardians of Eden, as an image form hovering over the Ark of the Covenant and decorating Solomon's temple, as the chariot of Jehovah, and surrounding God's throne.

We have already mentioned the cherub protecting the entrance to the Garden of Eden, so let's look at the Cherubim that hovered over the Ark of the Covenant and decorated the walls of Solomon's temple.

Ark of the Covenant & Solomon's Temple

When God gave instructions to Moses about the building of the Ark of the Covenant and the Tabernacle, He included cherubim. Likewise, when He gave instructions as to what Solomon's temple should look like, He included cherubim. Let's first look at the Ark of the Covenant.

When God made His covenant with the Israelite people, He promised good to them and the generations to follow if they obeyed Him and His laws. We know these laws as the Ten Commandments given to Moses on Mount Sinai. When the Ten Commandments were brought down from the mountain, God had the Israelites build a special box to keep them in. This box, or ark as it was called, was made of acacia wood and overlaid with pure gold and became known as the Ark of the Covenant. It was kept in the inner sanctum of the tabernacle until being moved to its more permanent home in the temple in Jerusalem. According to Hebrews 9:4, the Ark of the Covenant contained three items - the Ten Commandments, Aaron's staff that had budded, and a gold jar of manna.

The top of the ark was known as the "mercy seat". In Hebrew, it meant to cover or make atonement for. Once a year, the high priest would enter the Holy of Holies where the Ark was kept and make atonement for the sins of the Hebrew people. He did this before the mercy seat of the Ark of the Covenant. Why? Because the Ark of the Covenant served as a physical manifestation of God on earth. This was the place it was believed that God met with Moses and later the high priests of the temple.

So, where do the Cherubim come into play with the

Ark of the Covenant? In Exodus chapter 25 we find God's instructions to Moses on the construction of the Ark.

You shall make a mercy seat of pure gold;
two and a half cubits shall be its length and
a cubit and a half its width. And you shall
make two cherubim of gold; of hammered
work you shall make them at the two ends of
the mercy seat. Make one cherub at one end,
and the other cherub at the other end; you
shall make the cherubim at the two ends of
it of one piece with the mercy seat. And the
cherubim shall stretch out their wings above,
covering the mercy seat with their wings,
and they shall face one another; the faces of
the cherubim shall be toward the mercy seat.

Exodus 25:17-20

So that is the first place we see Cherubim in the sanctuary is atop the Ark of the Covenant. But God also included them throughout the temple.

Looking at 1 Kings chapter 6, we find documentation of Solomon building the first temple in Jerusalem. God was very specific in His instructions as to how this was to take place and what was to be included. In 1 Kings 6:19-22, we find Solomon building the inner sanctuary. Then, starting in verse 23, we find Solomon finishing out the inner sanctuary as well as the remainder of the temple. Let's look at what the Bible says here about Solomon's work.

So Solomon built the temple and finished it.
And he built the inside walls of the temple

*with cedar boards; from the floor of the tem-
ple to the ceiling he paneled the inside with
wood; and he covered the floor of the temple
with planks of cypress. Then he built the
twenty-cubit room at the rear of the temple, from floor to ceiling, with cedar boards;
he built it inside as the inner sanctuary, as
the Most Holy Place. And in front of it the
temple sanctuary was forty cubits long. The
inside of the temple was cedar, carved with
ornamental buds and open flowers. All was
cedar; there was no stone to be seen.
And he prepared the inner sanctuary inside
the temple, to set the ark of the covenant of
the LORD there. The inner sanctuary was
twenty cubits long, twenty cubits wide, and
twenty cubits high. He overlaid it with pure
gold, and overlaid the altar of cedar. So Solomon overlaid the inside of the temple with
pure gold. He stretched gold chains across the
front of the inner sanctuary, and overlaid it
with gold. The whole temple he overlaid with
gold, until he had finished all the temple; also
he overlaid with gold the entire altar that was
by the inner sanctuary.
Inside the inner sanctuary he made two
cherubim of olive wood, each ten cubits high.
One wing of the cherub was five cubits, and
the other wing of the cherub five cubits: ten
cubits from the tip of one wing to the tip
of the other. And the other cherub was ten
cubits; both cherubim were of the same size
and shape. The height of one cherub was ten
cubits, and so was the other cherub. Then he
set the cherubim inside the inner room; and*

they stretched out the wings of the cherubim
so that the wing of the one touched one wall,
and the wing of the other cherub touched the
other wall. And their wings touched each
other in the middle of the room. Also he overlaid the cherubim with gold.
Then he carved all the walls of the temple all
around, both the inner and outer sanctuaries,
with carved figures of cherubim, palm trees,
and open flowers. And the floor of the temple he overlaid with gold, both the inner and
outer sanctuaries.
For the entrance of the inner sanctuary he
made doors of olive wood; the lintel and
doorposts were one-fifth of the wall. The two
doors were of olive wood; and he carved on
them figures of cherubim, palm trees, and
open flowers, and overlaid them with gold;
and he spread gold on the cherubim and on
the palm trees. So for the door of the sanctuary he also made doorposts of olive wood,
one-fourth of the wall. And the two doors
were of cypress wood; two panels comprised
one folding door, and two panels comprised
the other folding door. Then he carved cherubim, palm trees, and open flowers on them,
and overlaid them with gold applied evenly
on the carved work.
And he built the inner court with three rows
of hewn stone and a row of cedar beams.
In the fourth year the foundation of the house
of the LORD was laid, in the month of Ziv.
And in the eleventh year, in the month of
Bul, which is the eighth month, the house
was finished in all its details and according to

all its plans. So he was seven years in build-
ing it.

1 Kings 6:14-38

Could you just imagine, two golden Angels, Cherubim specifically, fifteen feet high with their wings reaching out and touching one another? That must have been an incredible sight. Not only in the inner sanctuary, but also throughout the entire temple, Cherubim were part of the decorative elements.

As is becoming clearer to us, Cherubim have a special place in God's heart. Whenever we see a place where God meets with man, we find Cherubim. Why would this be? To answer that question, let's look at the next two places we find Cherubim.

Chariots of the Almighty

Psalm 18:10 reads.

And He rode upon a cherub, and flew;
He flew upon the wings of the wind.

And in Psalm 104:3 we find.

Who makes the clouds His chariot,
Who walks on the wings of the wind,

As we discussed in a previous chapter, angels are often associated with, and described as the wind. These verses lead us to believe that Cherubim serve as God's chariot. They carry the Almighty wherever He desires.

It is Ezekiel that gives us the best description of the Cherubim, as well as their role as God's chariot. In the book of Ezekiel, we find Ezekiel telling us about his vision of God. In chapter one, he gives us a very detailed description of Cherubim that pushes the limits of human imagination.

Now it came to pass in the thirtieth year, in the fourth month, on the fifth day of the month, as I was among the captives by the River Chebar, that the heavens were opened and I saw visions of God. On the fifth day of the month, which was in the fifth year of King Jehoiachin's captivity, the word of the LORD came expressly to Ezekiel the priest, the son of Buzi, in the land of the Chaldeans by the River Chebar; and the hand of the LORD was upon him there. Then I looked, and behold, a whirlwind was coming out of the north, a great cloud with raging fire engulfing itself; and brightness was all around it and radiating out of its midst like the color of amber, out of the midst of the fire. Also from within it came the likeness of four living creatures. And this was their appearance: they had the likeness of a man. Each one had four faces, and each one had four wings. Their legs were straight, and the soles of their feet were like the soles of calves' feet. They sparkled like the color of burnished bronze. The hands of a man were under their

*wings on their four sides; and each of the four
had faces and wings. Their wings touched
one another. The creatures did not turn when
they went, but each one went straight forward.
As for the likeness of their faces, each had the
face of a man; each of the four had the face of
a lion on the right side, each of the four had
the face of an ox on the left side, and each of
the four had the face of an eagle. Thus were
their faces. Their wings stretched upward;
two wings of each one touched one another,
and two covered their bodies. And each one
went straight forward; they went wherever
the spirit wanted to go, and they did not turn
when they went.
As for the likeness of the living creatures,
their appearance was like burning coals of
fire, like the appearance of torches going back
and forth among the living creatures. The fire
was bright, and out of the fire went lightning.
And the living creatures ran back and forth,
in appearance like a flash of lightning.
Now as I looked at the living creatures,
behold, a wheel was on the earth beside
each living creature with its four faces. The
appearance of the wheels and their workings
was like the color of beryl, and all four had
the same likeness. The appearance of their
workings was, as it were, a wheel in the middle of a wheel. When they moved, they went
toward any one of four directions; they did
not turn aside when they went. As for their
rims, they were so high they were awesome;
and their rims were full of eyes, all around*

*the four of them. When the living creatures
went, the wheels went beside them; and when
the living creatures were lifted up from the
earth, the wheels were lifted up. Wherever
the spirit wanted to go, they went, because
there the spirit went; and the wheels were
lifted together with them, for the spirit of the
living creatures was in the wheels. When
those went, these went; when those stood,
these stood; and when those were lifted up
from the earth, the wheels were lifted up
together with them, for the spirit of the living
creatures was in the wheels.*

*The likeness of the firmament above the heads
of the living creatures was like the color of
an awesome crystal, stretched out over their
heads. And under the firmament their wings
spread out straight, one toward another. Each
one had two which covered one side, and each
one had two which covered the other side of
the body. When they went, I heard the noise
of their wings, like the noise of many waters,
like the voice of the Almighty, a tumult like
the noise of an army; and when they stood
still, they let down their wings. A voice came
from above the firmament that was over their
heads; whenever they stood, they let down
their wings*

Following this vivid description of the angels, Ezekiel
tells us that above them was the throne of God with all
His glory.

And above the firmament over their heads
was the likeness of a throne, in appearance
like a sapphire stone; on the likeness of the
throne was a likeness with the appearance
of a man high above it. ²⁷ Also from the
appearance of His waist and upward I saw,
as it were, the color of amber with the appear-
ance of fire all around within it; and from
the appearance of His waist and downward
I saw, as it were, the appearance of fire with
brightness all around. ²⁸ Like the appear-
ance of a rainbow in a cloud on a rainy day,
so was the appearance of the brightness all
around it. This was the appearance of the
likeness of the glory of the LORD.

Ezekiel 1

Ezekiel continues describing the Glory of God and the
Cherubim in chapter 10. It is here that he firms up the idea
of the Cherubim being the Chariot of God.

And I looked, and there in the firmament that
was above the head of the cherubim, there
appeared something like a sapphire stone,
having the appearance of the likeness of a
throne.

Ezekiel 10:1

Then the glory of the LORD departed from
the threshold of the temple and stood over

the cherubim. And the cherubim lifted their wings and mounted up from the earth in my sight. When they went out, the wheels were beside them; and they stood at the door of the east gate of the LORD's house, and the glory of the God of Israel was above them.

This is the living creature I saw under the God of Israel by the River Chebar, and I knew they were cherubim.

Ezekiel 10:18-20

From Ezekiel's vision we see that whenever God is on the move, we find the Cherubim with Him. However, it is not only when God is moving that we find them. We also find them surrounding His throne in Heaven.

Surrounding God's Throne

Psalm 80, 99, and Samuel 4 all indicate that God is *"He that sitteth between the cherubim."*

Revelation 4:6 describes "four living creatures." These four creatures have the same visual characteristics as the Cherubim we find in Ezekiel's vision.

Before the throne there was a sea of glass, like crystal. And in the midst of the throne, and around the throne, were four living creatures full of eyes in front and in back. The first living creature was like a lion, the second living

creature like a calf, the third living creature
had a face like a man, and the fourth living
creature was like a flying eagle. The four
living creatures, each having six wings, were
full of eyes around and within. And they do
not rest day or night, saying:
"Holy, holy, holy,
Lord God Almighty,
Who was and is and is to come!

Revelation 4:6-8

The Cherubim have the distinct privilege of being in God's presence continuously. They surround Him as He is on His throne in Heaven, and they serve as His chariot carrying Him wherever He desires.

It is no wonder that God in His instructions to Moses and Solomon would include them in the design and decoration of His most Holy objects and places.

Cherubim are far more than cute little angels that we see decorating valentine's boxes each year. They are mighty angels that stand guard over the Garden of Eden, adorn the Ark of the Covenant, guard the Holy of Holies, decorate the walls of Solomon's temple, serve as the Lord's chariot, and stand in awe around His throne saying

Holy, holy, holy, Lord God Almighty,

Who was and is and is to come!

CHAPTER EIGHT

SERAPHIM

The Seraphim are the fiery burning ones that were created for a specific purpose. The word Seraphim means fiery ones. It is the plural word for Seraph. We know little about the Seraphim except what is written in Isaiah. Isaiah chapter six is the only place in the Bible that mentions the Seraphim by name. They must be in a similar class of angels to the Cherubim, because they share many of the same characteristics. Let's start our look at the Seraphim by turning to Isaiah.

Isaiah is being given a vision by God. In this vision, he sees God in the Temple. You may remember that this is where God rode on the Cherubim. In this same vision, Isaiah also sees the Seraphim.

In the year that King Uzziah died, I saw the
Lord sitting on a throne, high and lifted up,
and the train of His robe filled the temple.
Above it stood seraphim; each one had six
wings: with two he covered his face, with
two he covered his feet, and with two he flew.
And one cried to another and said:

"Holy, holy, holy is the LORD of hosts;
The whole earth is full of His glory!"
And the posts of the door were shaken by the
voice of him who cried out, and the house
was filled with smoke.

Isaiah 6:1-4

That must have been an amazing sight. God in all His glory, sitting on His throne and the train of His robe filling the entire temple. The temple was massive. Then above Him stood the magnificent Seraphim with six wings chanting, *"Holy, holy, holy is the Lord of hosts…"*. What an awe-inspiring vision that must have been.

Let's talk about those wings for a minute. Isaiah said that the Seraphim had six wings. With two he covered his face, with two he covered his feet, and with two he flew. First, notice that Isaiah calls the Seraph "he." This leads us to believe that the Seraphim must in some way resemble man because Isaiah recognized him as "he". This supports what we talked about previously about angels being masculine.

With one set of wings, he covered his face. Bible scholars believe that this is out of reverence to God and to shield themselves from God's brilliance. Even the Seraphim don't feel worthy to look at God with their own eyes. Not to mention that God's glory shines so bright that in the New Jerusalem, there will be no need for sunlight, because His glory is so bright that it lights all of existence. Therefore, it stands to reason that the Seraphim that are above God's throne might need to shield their eyes.

With another set of wings, he covered his feet. Why would he cover his feet? Do you remember when Moses went up on the mountain to meet with God? He was told to remove his sandals because the ground he was standing on was holy ground. Think of how holy the area around the Lord's throne must be. So out of the same respect and reverence, the Seraphim cover their feet.

With another set of wings, he flew. This passage verifies that some angels do indeed have wings for the express purpose of flying and moving about.

What about what they were saying? *"Holy, holy, holy is the Lord of hosts..."* The important thing to notice in this passage is the triple repetition of the word holy. In the Hebrew language, this was done to emphasize an idea. For instance, when Jesus spoke, He often said "Verily, verily I say unto you." The double word usage of "verily" was done to place emphasis and importance on what was about to be said. It is sort of like saying "far far away." We say that to emphasize that something is very far away. To say *"holy, holy, holy..."* is to say that the Lord is very, very, very holy.

Isaiah goes on to tell of how he felt unworthy to be witnessing such a thing and to be looking at God on His throne. His sin made him unclean, and therefore unworthy. Look what happened next.

So I said:
"Woe is me, for I am undone!
Because I am a man of unclean lips,
And I dwell in the midst of a people of
unclean lips;
For my eyes have seen the King,
The LORD of hosts."
Then one of the seraphim flew to me, having
in his hand a live coal which he had taken
with the tongs from the altar. And he touched
my mouth with it, and said:
"Behold, this has touched your lips;

Your iniquity is taken away,
And your sin purged."

Isaiah 6:1-7

In this instance, we see that the Seraphim were more than just choir members in God's throne room. They also acted as purging agents to cleanse Isaiah of his sinfulness. Only God can forgive and cleanse sin. For Isaiah, this cleansing came through the actions of the Seraphim.

We have already mentioned that Isaiah chapter six is the only place in the Bible that mentions the Seraphim by name. However, that may not be the only place in the Bible where we see them. In Revelation chapter four, we see the four living creatures. These creatures are described as having six wings like the Seraphim described in Isaiah chapter 6. In addition, the four living creatures are saying the same verse, *"Holy, holy, holy is the Lord God Almighty..."* Let's look at Revelation 4.

After these things I looked, and behold, a
door standing open in heaven. And the first
voice which I heard was like a trumpet speak-
ing with me, saying, "Come up here, and I
will show you things which must take place
after this."
Immediately I was in the Spirit; and behold,
a throne set in heaven, and One sat on the
throne. And He who sat there was like a
jasper and a sardius stone in appearance;
and there was a rainbow around the throne,
in appearance like an emerald. Around the
throne were twenty-four thrones, and on
the thrones I saw twenty-four elders sitting,

*clothed in white robes; and they had crowns
of gold on their heads. And from the throne
proceeded lightnings, thunderings, and
voices. Seven lamps of fire were burning
before the throne, which are the seven Spirits
of God.
Before the throne there was a sea of glass, like
crystal. And in the midst of the throne, and
around the throne, were four living creatures
full of eyes in front and in back. The first living creature was like a lion, the second living
creature like a calf, the third living creature
had a face like a man, and the fourth living
creature was like a flying eagle. The four
living creatures, each having six wings, were
full of eyes around and within. And they do
not rest day or night, saying:
"Holy, holy, holy,
Lord God Almighty,
Who was and is and is to come!"*

Revelation 4:1-8

Some believe that the four living creatures are distinct from the other angelic beings. However, when looking at their physical description, one notices that they have similar attributes to the Cherubim. Their faces are like different creatures. On the other hand, the fact that they have six wings points to the fact that the four living creatures could be Seraphim. In addition to the physical characteristics of the Seraphim, they are found repeating the same verse. Both facts lead many Bible scholars to believe that the Four Living Creatures are Seraphim.

We are talking about angels and most believe that the Seraphim are a special order of angels; but what if they were not angels at all? Could it be possible that they are an entirely separate creature created by God for their specific purpose? Let's go back to the book of Revelation and read about the Lamb Opening the Scroll.

And I saw in the right hand of Him who sat on the throne a scroll written inside and on the back, sealed with seven seals. Then I saw a strong angel proclaiming with a loud voice, "Who is worthy to open the scroll and to loose its seals?" And no one in heaven or on the earth or under the earth was able to open the scroll, or to look at it.
So I wept much, because no one was found worthy to open and read the scroll, or to look at it. But one of the elders said to me, "Do not weep. Behold, the Lion of the tribe of Judah, the Root of David, has prevailed to open the scroll and to loose its seven seals." And I looked, and behold, in the midst of the throne and of the four living creatures, and in the midst of the elders, stood a Lamb as though it had been slain, having seven horns and seven eyes, which are the seven Spirits of God sent out into all the earth. Then He came and took the scroll out of the right hand of Him who sat on the throne.
Worthy Is the Lamb
Now when He had taken the scroll, the four living creatures and the twenty-four elders fell down before the Lamb, each having a harp, and golden bowls full of incense, which are the prayers of the saints. And they sang a

new song, saying:
"You are worthy to take the scroll,
And to open its seals;
For You were slain,
And have redeemed us to God by Your blood
Out of every tribe and tongue and people and
nation,
And have made us kings and priests to our
God;
And we shall reign on the earth."
Then I looked, and I heard the voice of many
angels around the throne, the living crea-
tures, and the elders; and the number of them
was ten thousand times ten thousand, and
thousands of thousands, aying with a loud
voice:
"Worthy is the Lamb who was slain
To receive power and riches and wisdom,
And strength and honor and glory and
blessing!"

Revelation 5:1-12

Now, look closely at verse 11.

Then I looked, and I heard the voice of many
angels around the throne, the living crea-
tures, and the elders; and the number of them
was ten thousand times ten thousand, and
thousands of thousands, saying with a loud
voice:
"Worthy is the Lamb who was slain
To receive power and riches and wisdom,

And strength and honor and glory and
blessing!"

The Four Living Creatures which are thought to be Seraphim are distinguished from the rest of the angels. Like
the elders, they are listed separately. Is this just a coinci-
dence or might it imply that Seraphim are not angels as
we know them, but a separate and distinct celestial being
of their own? If this is the case with the Seraphim, could
it also apply to the Cherubim?

CHAPTER NINE

THE ANGEL OF THE LORD

Before all time. Before anything was, there existed one who would take the form of a singular angel. He stood with majesty and glory beside God the Father. He reached out His hand, and spoke creation into existence. As the other angels began to take form, He was there. As the universe came into existence, He was there. As the earth took shape and became inhabited by man, He was there. This angel always has been and always will be. He says in the book of Revelation that He is the Alpha and the Omega, the Beginning, and the End. The Bible tells us that by Him all things were made. Other angels have taken the form of humans, but He is the only one to have ever become one. Other angels have come to visit man, but He is the only one to have ever come to redeem man. Other angels stand at God's throne, but He sits at God's right hand. As magnificent as other angels are, none compare to the Angel of the Lord.

The Angel of the Lord is probably the most mysterious yet obvious angel in the Bible. Most scripture simply alludes to whom this angel is; leaving for us a mystery of sorts. There are Old and New Testament references to "angels of the Lord," "an angel of the Lord," and "the angel of the

Lord." The article "the" refers to a specific being separate from the other angels. It seems that when the article "the" is used, the Bible is referring to this special angel that we know as The Angel of the Lord.

What most people ponder when reading the scriptures is, who The Angel of the Lord is. The Bible is clear on who Michael and Gabriel are, but is it clear on who the Angel of the Lord is? The answer to that question is sometimes. When speaking of the Lord, one could be referring to any third of the Trinity, God the Father, God the Son, or God the Holy Spirit. All are one, yet each has its part and identity. In the case of The Angel of the Lord, most bible scholars believe that this special identity belongs to Jesus, God the Son.

In this chapter, I would like to point out six reasons that we can be assured that the title The Angel of the Lord belongs to Jesus.

Reason 1

Because Jesus says that He has always existed.

When we think of the life of Jesus, we tend to think of it in terms of His earthly life. We also tend to think of a future in heaven with Jesus. However, we rarely think of Jesus' life before He was incarnated here on this earth. John makes it clear in John 1 that Jesus' life has always been. There he says.

In the beginning was the Word, and the
Word was with God, and the Word was God.

*He was in the beginning with God. All things
were made through Him, and without Him
nothing was made that was made. In Him
was life, and the life was the light of men.
And the light shines in the darkness, and the
darkness did not comprehend it.*

John 1:1-5

Jesus has always existed. Even before time and creation, He existed. It is hard for us to comprehend this given the fact that we as humans operate in a linear form of time, given to a past and a future that began at a particular instant. But Jesus' life has not and will not be like that. He made this point when talking with the Pharisees one day in the temple.

Jesus was teaching in the temple when the Pharisees accused Him of bearing witness of Himself, claiming that it was not true. Jesus then goes through a long discussion on how His witness is true and is from the Father. The discussion gets rather heated. John tells us how it ended in John chapter 8.

*Your father Abraham rejoiced to see My day,
and he saw it and was glad.*

*Then the Jews said to Him, "You are not
yet fifty years old, and have You seen Abraham?"
Jesus said to them, "Most assuredly, I say to
you, before Abraham was, I AM."*

John 8:57-58

Jesus makes it very clear to the Pharisees and us that His existence has not been limited to time as we know it. You may agree that Jesus has always existed, but still wonder how this could have anything to do with The Angel of the Lord. Many people spend years reading the Bible but never make this connection. Allow me to explain.

The Angel of the Lord has played a major role throughout the history of mankind. Scattered throughout the Old Testament are passages that indicate that He was not only there, but played a vital role in how history unfolded. Because Jesus has always existed and has been with mankind since the very beginning, doesn't it make sense that He would play a vital role in its history? After all, this is His kingdom. Why shouldn't He not only play a vital role, but be among His people in the process? Because Jesus was not yet incarnated as the Christ, the vehicle for Him to play His role and be among His people was through The Angel of the Lord.

Reason 2

The Angel of the Lord accepted worship. Regular angels do not.

In Judges chapter 6, we find the Israelites under oppression from the Midianites. Each year when the Israelite harvest would become ready, the Midianites and several other hostile neighbors would come into the land, taking what they could for themselves and destroying what was left. Almost nothing was left for the Israelites themselves. A man named Gideon, who was the least of his family in a clan that was considered the least of the Israelites, was hiding in a wine press, threshing what grain he could hide. As he was threshing the wheat and pondering the poor conditions the Lord had left them in, The Angel of the Lord appeared to him with a message. The message was for him to go in the name of the Lord and defeat the Midianites. After some back and forth, Gideon realizes the man he is talking to is The Angel of the Lord. Gideon is so honored by this visit that he asks to be allowed to bring an offering.

Do not depart from here, I pray, until I come to You and bring out my offering and set it before You."
And He said, "I will wait until you come back."
So Gideon went in and prepared a young goat, and unleavened bread from an ephah of flour. The meat he put in a basket, and he put the broth in a pot; and he brought them out to Him under the terebinth tree and presented them. The Angel of God said to him, "Take the meat and the unleavened bread and lay them on this rock, and pour out the broth."
And he did so.
Then the Angel of the LORD put out the end of the staff that was in His hand, and touched the meat and the unleavened bread; and fire rose out of the rock and consumed the meat and the unleavened bread. And the Angel of the LORD departed out of his sight.

Judges 6:18-21

The Angel of the Lord accepted Gideon's offering. After which, Gideon went on to defeat the Midianites in the name of the Lord.

This is not the only place in the book of Judges where we find The Angel of the Lord accepting an offering of worship. Another occurrence is with a man named Manoah.

You may not be familiar with who Manoah was, but you are probably familiar with a man named Samson. The same Samson that had long hair, a stubborn side, superhuman strength, and was used by God in a mighty way. Manoah was Samson's daddy.

The Israelites had been under the thumb of the Philistines for forty years when The Angel of the Lord appeared to Manoah and his wife with news about a baby that would be born to them. This was amazing news because Manoah's wife had been barren all her life.

The Angel of the Lord gave them specific instructions about her pregnancy and how the child would be raised. He then He made it clear to them that the child would be used by God in mighty ways to free the Israelite people from the hands of the Philistines.

Like Gideon, Manoah wanted to offer praise and worship to The Angel of the Lord through an offering. Judges chapter 13 tells the story.

> *Then Manoah said to the Angel of the LORD, "Please let us detain You, and we will prepare a young goat for You."*
> *And the Angel of the LORD said to Manoah, "Though you detain Me, I will not eat your food. But if you offer a burnt offering, you must offer it to the LORD." (For Manoah did not know He was the Angel of the LORD.)*
> *Then Manoah said to the Angel of the*

*LORD, "What is Your name, that when
Your words come to pass we may honor
You?"
And the Angel of the LORD said to him,
"Why do you ask My name, seeing it is won-
derful?"
So Manoah took the young goat with the
grain offering, and offered it upon the rock
to the LORD. And He did a wondrous thing
while Manoah and his wife looked on— it
happened as the flame went up toward
heaven from the altar—the Angel of the
LORD ascended in the flame of the altar!
When Manoah and his wife saw this, they
fell on their faces to the ground. When the
Angel of the LORD appeared no more to
Manoah and his wife, then Manoah knew
that He was the Angel of the LORD.
And Manoah said to his wife, "We shall
surely die, because we have seen God!"
But his wife said to him, "If the LORD had
desired to kill us, He would not have accepted
a burnt offering and a grain offering from
our hands, nor would He have shown us all
these things, nor would He have told us such
things as these at this time."*

Judges 13:15-23

These are just two examples of how The Angel of the
Lord accepted praise and worship from men. How does
this prove that The Angel of the Lord is Jesus you ask? It
proves it because no created being is worthy of receiving
such offerings. There is only one who is worthy of praise
and worship, and that is our Lord. Revelation 5:11- 14 tells

us that untold angels, heavenly beings, and all of creation declare it so.

> *Then I looked, and I heard the voice of many*
> *angels around the throne, the living creatures,*
> *and the elders; and the number of them was*
> *ten thousand times ten thousand, and thou-*
> *sands of thousands, saying with a loud voice:*
> *"Worthy is the Lamb who was slain*
> *To receive power and riches and wisdom,*
> *And strength and honor and glory and bless-*
> *ing!"*
> *And every creature which is in heaven and*
> *on the earth and under the earth and such as*
> *are in the sea, and all that are in them, I heard*
> *saying:*
> *"Blessing and honor and glory and power*
> *Be to Him who sits on the throne,*
> *And to the Lamb, forever and ever!"*
> *Then the four living creatures said, "Amen!"*
> *And the twenty-four elders fell down and*
> *worshiped Him who lives forever and ever.*
>
> *Revelation 5:11-14*

By accepting the praise and offerings of Gideon and Manoah, The Angel of the Lord shows Himself to be none other than our Lord and Savior. Why does that prove that He is not just an ordinary angel? Because as magnificent as angels are, they are still created beings formed from the very words of God the Father; and as such, are not worthy of praise, worship, or any other offering that could be given. The elect angels of God understand this and cannot accept praise or worship from any other created being. We see proof of this in the book of Revelation. Throughout the book, John goes through a process of being shown many amazing things. At one point in this process, he is guided by an angel. John is so overwhelmed with awe that he feels the need to bow down to this angel. Listen to what the angel says to him.

> *And I fell at his feet to worship him. But he said to me, "See that you do not do that! I am your fellow servant, and of your brethren who have the testimony of Jesus. Worship God! For the testimony of Jesus is the spirit of prophecy."*
>
> *Revelation 19:10*

Angels do many things well, but probably the thing they do best is to point to God. The angel made it clear to John and us that angels are our fellow servants and only the Lord is to be praised.

Reason 3

Those who saw the Angel of the Lord feared for their lives.

In Exodus 33, Moses has gone up onto the mountain to be with God and beg forgiveness for the sins of the Israelite people. During this meeting, God commands Moses to leave Sinai and begin the journey toward the promised land. Upon his return to camp, Moses erects his tent outside the camp and calls it the Tabernacle of Meeting. Whenever Moses would enter the tabernacle, God would meet with him there and they would talk. During one of these meetings, Moses asks God to show him His glory.

And he said, "Please, show me Your glory." Then He said, "I will make all My goodness pass before you, and I will proclaim the name of the LORD before you. I will be gracious to whom I will be gracious, and I will have compassion on whom I will have compassion." But He said, "You cannot see My face; for no man shall see Me, and live." And the LORD said, "Here is a place by Me, and you shall stand on the rock. So it shall be, while My glory passes by, that I will put you in the cleft of the rock, and will cover you with My hand while I pass by. Then I will take away My hand, and you shall see My back; but My face shall not be seen."

Exodus 33:18-23

Because of what is recorded in verse 20, *"You cannot see My face; for no man shall see Me, and live"*, Jewish people throughout the Bible believed that if they were to see the face of God that they would die. Gideon as well as Manoah and his wife were fearful of just that.

Judges 6 tells us of Gideon's fear.

Now Gideon perceived that He was the Angel of the LORD. So Gideon said, "Alas, O Lord GOD! For I have seen the Angel of

the LORD face to face."
Then the LORD said to him, "Peace be
with you; do not fear, you shall not die." So
Gideon built an altar there to the LORD, and
called it The-LORD-Is-Peace.

Judges 6:22-24

Judges 13 tells us of Manoah's fear.

When the Angel of the LORD appeared no
more to Manoah and his wife, then Manoah
knew that He was the Angel of the LORD.
And Manoah said to his wife, "We shall
surely die, because we have seen God!"
But his wife said to him, "If the LORD had
desired to kill us, He would not have accepted
a burnt offering and a grain offering from
our hands, nor would He have shown us all
these things, nor would He have told us such
things as these at this time."

Judges 13:21-23

Had The Angel of the Lord been an ordinary angel, neither Gideon, Manoah, nor his wife would have feared for their lives. They were all given a supernatural awareness that this was not just an ordinary angel but the Lord Himself.

Reason 4

The Angel of the Lord spoke with the authority of God.

Each time we find The Angel of the Lord in scripture, we find Him bringing a message to those He visits. Each one of these messages is spoken with the authority of God. How is that different from messages that ordinary angels bring? The elect angels, ordinary angels, speak their messages "by" the authority of God. The Angel of the Lord speaks His messages "with" the authority of God. Let's look at some examples to clarify this.

When in scripture we find ordinary angels giving messages to humans it is usually clear that they have been sent by God with that message. For example, in Genesis 19 we find that God has had all he can stand of the sin of the people of Sodom and Gomorrah. He has chosen to wipe these cities from existence. However, He remembers Abraham and sends His angels to Lot warning him of the destruction to come. Verses 12-13 record what the angels said to Lot.

> Then the men said to Lot, "Have you any-
> one else here? Son-in-law, your sons, your
> daughters, and whomever you have in the
> city—take them out of this place! For we will
> destroy this place, because the outcry against
> them has grown great before the face of the

LORD, and the LORD has sent us to destroy it."

Genesis 19:12-13

The last part of verse 13 is clear. *"the Lord has sent us..."* It is clear that these angels were sent with a message and a job to do "by" the authority of God. Let's now look at an example of The Angel of the Lord bringing His message "with" the authority of God.

Abram and Sarai have become old and still have no son to carry on the legacy of Abram. Sarai decides that because of this, Abram should have a child with her maidservant so that Abram's family legacy might continue. Sarai's maidservant was Hagar, who indeed became pregnant with Abram's child. Once pregnant, Hagar began to despise Sarai. As a result, Sarai was harsh to her and forced her to flee. Genesis 16 picks up the story from here.

Now the Angel of the LORD found her by a spring of water in the wilderness, by the spring on the way to Shur. And He said, "Hagar, Sarai's maid, where have you come from, and where are you going?"
She said, "I am fleeing from the presence of my mistress Sarai."
The Angel of the LORD said to her, "Return to your mistress, and submit yourself under her hand."

Then the Angel of the LORD said to her, "I will multiply your descendants exceedingly, so that they shall not be counted for

multitude." And the Angel of the LORD said
to her:
"Behold, you are with child,
And you shall bear a son.
You shall call his name Ishmael,
Because the LORD has heard your affliction.
He shall be a wild man;
His hand shall be against every man,
And every man's hand against him.
And he shall dwell in the presence of all his
brethren."

Genesis 16:10-12

Notice in verse 10 The Angel of the Lord says *"I will multiply…"* Had this been an ordinary angel, he would have said "The Lord shall multiply…"

We can go back to the story of Gideon to see another example. Remember when The Angel of the Lord comes to Gideon while he is hiding in the wine press and delivers to him the message that he would be the one to defeat the Midianite oppressors? Gideon is questioning how he could be the one God would choose to do such a mighty task when he is the least of all the Israelite men. Listen to what The Angel of the Lord says to him.

And the Angel of the LORD appeared to him,
and said to him, "The LORD is with you,
you mighty man of valor!"
Gideon said to Him, "O my lord, if the
LORD is with us, why then has all this hap-
pened to us? And where are all His miracles
which our fathers told us about, saying, 'Did
not the LORD bring us up from Egypt?' But

now the LORD has forsaken us and delivered
us into the hands of the Midianites."
Then the LORD turned to him and said, "Go
in this might of yours, and you shall save
Israel from the hand of the Midianites. Have
I not sent you?"
So he said to Him, "O my Lord, how can I
save Israel? Indeed my clan is the weakest in
Manasseh, and I am the least in my father's
house."
And the LORD said to him, "Surely I will be
with you, and you shall defeat the Midianites
as one man."

Judges 6:12-16

Did you catch that last part? In verse 16, The Angel of the Lord says, *"Surely I will be with you."* Had it been an ordinary angel speaking with Gideon, he would have said "Surely the Lord will be with you", but instead He says "I" will be with you.

In both these examples, we see The Angel of the Lord speaking with the authority that only God possesses. Not "by" that authority, but "with" that authority.

Reason 5

The appearances of The Angel of the Lord cease after the incarnation of Christ.

Every Christmas in Christian homes and churches throughout the world we hear the reading of the Christmas story in Luke chapter 2. This sweet story tells of how Joseph and Mary settled into a small stable meant for cattle and sheep and there brought our savior into this world. The angels in Heaven rejoiced and proclaimed to the shepherds this glorious event. Christ's birth meant many things to many people, but one thing that is hardly noticed is that with His birth came the end of the appearances of The Angel of the Lord.

If one thinks about it, it makes perfect sense. The Angel of the Lord was Christ's vehicle to be among His people and to be a part of their lives. His birth as a man meant that He would walk among us in His kingdom. He no longer needed to appear as an angel because He was appearing as a man; to live with us, talk with us, laugh with us, and die for us. This point of The Angel of the Lord ceasing to appear after Christ's incarnation can be a confusing matter because of the language we use in translating the Bible.

Throughout the New Testament, we find references to "an angel of the Lord" and even "the angel of the Lord."

But while he thought about these things, behold, an angel of the Lord appeared to him in a dream, saying, "Joseph, son of David, do not be afraid to take to you Mary your wife, for that which is conceived in her is of the Holy Spirit.

Matthew 1:20

Now an angel of the Lord spoke to Philip, saying, "Arise and go toward the south along the road which goes down from Jerusalem to Gaza." This is desert.

Acts 8:26

*Now behold, an angel of the Lord stood by
him, and a light shone in the prison; and he
struck Peter on the side and raised him up,
saying, "Arise quickly!" And his chains fell
off his hands.*

Acts 12:7

*And behold, there was a great earthquake; for
an angel of the Lord descended from heaven,
and came and rolled back the stone from the
door, and sat on it.*

Matthew 28:2

All these verses refer to "an" angel of the Lord. This
seems clear enough to distinguish these angels from The
Angel of the Lord; however, these verses were taken from
the New King James Version of the Bible. If you were to look
them up in the King James Version, you would find that
the article "an" has been replaced with "the". This brings
some confusion into the matter because as we talked about
previously, whenever we find the article "the" is used in
conjunction with an angel of the Lord, it is usually referring
to The Angel of the Lord or Christ.

It is important to note that our modern-day Bibles, the
King James Version being one of them, were translated
from the original Greek manuscripts. In the original Greek
language, there are no articles of "an" and "the". Those were
placed by our modern translators so that the English translation could be understood by English readers. Therefore,
the use of "an" and "the" in reference to The Angel of the
Lord in the New Testament has no consequence.

When one stops to think on the matter it makes perfect sense that the appearances of The Angel of the Lord cease after the incarnation of Christ. Why would the Lord need to appear as an angel when He walked the Earth as a man? There was no need to appear to someone supernaturally, He simply walked up to them and started a conversation much like you and me.

Reason 6

He identified Himself.

I remember as a child in Sunday School hearing the story of Moses and the burning bush. There were pictures of Moses standing with his staff in his hand looking at a bush that was completely ablaze. Little did I know at the time, but this story reveals the true identity of The Angel of the Lord.

Now Moses was tending the flock of Jethro his father-in-law, the priest of Midian. And he led the flock to the back of the desert, and came to Horeb, the mountain of God. And the Angel of the LORD appeared to him in a flame of fire from the midst of a bush. So he looked, and behold, the bush was burning with fire, but the bush was not consumed. Then Moses said, "I will now turn aside and see this great sight, why the bush does not burn."

So when the LORD saw that he turned aside
to look, God called to him from the midst of
the bush and said, "Moses, Moses!"
And he said, "Here I am."
Then He said, "Do not draw near this place.
Take your sandals off your feet, for the place
where you stand is holy ground." Moreover
He said, "I am the God of your father—the
God of Abraham, the God of Isaac, and the
God of Jacob." And Moses hid his face, for he
was afraid to look upon God.

Exodus 3:1-6

In many places in the Bible, scripture tells us of The Angel of the Lord; but most often, we are left to interpret for ourselves the identity of this angel. This story however makes it as one of my professors used to say, "blatantly obvious to the most casual observer."

In verse 2, we see The Angel of the Lord identified in the burning bush. So, we know that it is He that Moses is having this conversation with. Then on in verse 6, we see that the scripture reveals that it is *the God of your father, the God of Abraham, the God of Isaac, and the God of Jacob."* Through this bit of scripture, the answer to the mystery is unveiled as we see God revealing to us that He is The Angel of the Lord.

CHAPTER TEN

MICHAEL THE ARCHANGEL

Many times, angels are painted as dainty creatures with their halos and long flowing robes. There may indeed be angels this way. Some angels in the Bible, however, are far from dainty. Some angels are warriors. When the Lord opened Gehazi's eyes so that he could see into the supernatural realm, he did not see dainty creatures. He saw angelic warriors prepared for battle. An angelic army so great that the entire surrounding mountains were filled with them. The book of Revelation is full of examples of angels that could hardly be called anything other than warriors. Chief among these angelic warriors would be an archangel.

The word "archangel" means angel of the highest order. It is a compound word made of two Greek words. The first is "archon" meaning "chief or ruler" and the second is "angelos" meaning "messenger or angel". Together the words form "archangel" which means "the chief of angels." Therefore, an archangel is the chief or leader of the angelic realm; the general of God's mighty angelic army. This would fit with the idea of an angelic hierarchy that is alluded to throughout the Bible. If there is a hierarchy, there must be a leader.

The word archangel appears in only two verses of the Bible. The first of the two verses is 1 Thessalonians 4:16. It reads.

> *For the Lord Himself will descend from heaven with a shout, with the voice of an archangel, and with the trumpet of God. And the dead in Christ will rise first.*

Paul is telling us that at some unknown hour in the future, it will be the voice of an archangel along with the trumpet of God that will sound when the Lord raptures His Church. I can't even imagine what that is going to sound like!

The second verse containing the word archangel is found in Jude 1:9. It reads.

> *Yet Michael the archangel, in contending with the devil, when he disputed about the body of Moses, dared not bring against him a reviling accusation, but said, "The Lord rebuke you!*

The one thing that you will hear me reiterate over and over is the fact that angels always demonstrate absolute dedication and unquestionable obedience to the Lord. This verse shows that in the way that Michael, the most powerful angel, did not rebuke the devil on his own accord but said *"The Lord rebuke you!"*. If Michael, the most powerful angel in Heaven looks to the Lord for his strength and power, shouldn't you and I do the same? There is a lot that you and I could learn from this verse.

An interesting thing about this verse is that it is the only place in the Bible where an archangel is named. Either Michael, whose name means "who is like God", is the only archangel there is, or he is the only one that God has chosen to tell us about. Some believe that Gabriel is an archangel. There is no doubt that Gabriel is an important angel, but nowhere in scripture is he identified as an archangel.

The mystery as to whether Michael is the sole archangel is deepened by looking at Daniel 10:13. It reads.

But the prince of the kingdom of Persia
withstood me twenty-one days; and behold,
Michael, one of the chief princes, came to
help me, for I had been left alone there with
the kings of Persia.

Michael is called *"one of the chief princes"*. This could indicate that there are other archangels since it puts Michael in the category of other chief princes. However, let me caution you not to mix words from the Bible with our limited understanding of some of their meanings. Michael is no doubt one of the chief princes because the scripture tells us that, but that does not necessarily mean that the other chief princes are archangels. Even if that were the case, the fact that God has chosen to only reveal Michael as an archangel would seem to indicate that he would be the leader even of that elite group. In short, when it comes to angels, Michael it seems is their leader.

I am sure that as an archangel Michael has many duties. Of these, we know very little except for the fact that one of those duties is spiritual warfare. Let's turn once again to

Daniel to see this firsthand. In Daniel 10 we find Daniel on the banks of the mighty Tigris River where he is visited by an angel. Daniel describes the angel starting in verse 5.

> *I lifted my eyes and looked, and behold, a certain man clothed in linen, whose waist was girded with gold of Uphaz! His body was like beryl, his face like the appearance of lightning, his eyes like torches of fire, his arms and feet like burnished bronze in color, and the sound of his words like the voice of a multitude.*

Daniel was so awe-struck by what he saw that all his strength left him. When the angel started to speak, Daniel fell to the ground face-first into a deep sleep. The next thing Daniel knows is that the angel touches him and helps him to his hands and knees as the trembling is removed from his body. When Daniel finally makes his way to his feet, the angel addresses him.

> *Then he said to me, "Do not fear, Daniel, for from the first day that you set your heart to understand, and to humble yourself before your God, your words were heard; and I have come because of your words. But the prince of the kingdom of Persia withstood me twenty-one days; and behold, Michael, one of the chief princes, came to help me, for I had been left alone there with the kings of Persia. Now I have come to make you understand what will happen to your people in the latter*

*days, for the vision refers to many days yet to
come."*

A little background information might be helpful here.
Daniel and his fellow Israelites have been taken captive by
King Nebuchadnezzar II and hauled off to Babylon. This
exile to Babylon was an instrument of judgment against
Israel for their idolatry and rebellion against the Lord.
Nevertheless, Daniel is praying for the deliverance of his
nation. It is somewhere around the year 536 BC and Zerub-
babel has left with some of the Jews to return to Jerusalem
in the hopes of rebuilding the city. Daniel, however, has
stayed behind in Babylon. That's where we find him here
in chapter 10.

Daniel is given a vision about things to come and is
praying over that vision and for his people when he is
visited by the angel on the banks of the Tigris. We know
from scripture that Daniel has been in a state of prayer and
mourning for some three weeks. It is interesting to note
here that the angel tells Daniel that he has been detained
for twenty-one days, which is three weeks. The angel also
explains that it was the prince of the kingdom of Persia that
detained him. Something that might be easy to miss here is
that Babylon is in Persia - both of which are in modern-day
Iran. Who is this prince of the kingdom of Persia? Most
likely, he is a fallen angel that has been given the task by
Satan of disrupting the government and mindset of the
nation of Persia. The angel that was sent to Daniel to explain
the vision was detained by this prince of Persia. So, we see
here that in the spiritual realm beyond our vision, there
is spiritual warfare being waged between Satan and his
demons and God's angelic army over the wellbeing of the
nations of our planet. This demon was so powerful that it
detained the angel for three full weeks. Finally, Michael,

the archangel comes to his aid. In my mind, I envision the demon and angel in an all-out battle with swords, fire, thunder, and all sorts of supernatural weapons when, to the demon's surprise, Michael appears and aids the angel in quickly dispatching him. I am sure the demon shook in fear and turned for home when Michael stepped on the scene, because he would have known exactly who Michael was. You see, Daniel 10:21 and Daniel 12:1 tell us that Michael is the prince of Israel. God has given the job of watching over His chosen nation to His most powerful angel - Michael.

Allow me the privilege of taking a side road here for just a moment. We are talking about spiritual warfare. The job of the prince of the kingdom of Persia was to, borrowing a cliche from *Star Wars*, turn that nation to the dark side. We see that God has allowed that. Persia is modern-day Iran. That part of the world was in turmoil in Daniel's day, and it is in turmoil today. So, the demonic forces that are identified as princes of certain nations seem to have the authority to sway their nations to the dark side. Look at Daniel 10:20.

> *Then he said, "Do you know why I have come to you? And now I must return to fight with the prince of Persia; and when I have gone forth, indeed the prince of Greece will come.*

After the angel fought with the prince of the kingdom of Persia, he battled the prince of Greece. This little tidbit of scripture usually gets glossed over but is an important message of prophecy from the angel. Why? Because interestingly, after Persia, Greece became the next world power and dominated Israel.

So, this whole discussion of spiritual warfare in Daniel makes one think about what must be taking place behind the scenes right now. Do we have angels fighting for the United States, or is it being influenced by some demonic power - a prince of the United States of America? Paul is quick to remind us through Ephesians 6:12 that it is not flesh and blood that we battle but says that we are at battle *"against principalities, against powers, against the rulers of the darkness of this age, against spiritual hosts of wickedness in the heavenly places."* This is even more reason our nation must rely on the Lord Almighty for protection.

Now back to the main road. We were talking about Michael and his role in spiritual warfare. We have seen from this example in Daniel that Michael assists the angels that are fighting on Israel's behalf. The Bible gives us two more examples of Michael's role in spiritual warfare, and they are found in Revelation 12:7-8 and Daniel 12:1.

Revelation 12:7-8 reads.

> *Now war arose in heaven, Michael and his angels fighting against the dragon. And the dragon and his angels fought back, but he was defeated, and there was no longer any place for them in heaven.*

And in Daniel 12:1 we have:

> *At that time Michael shall stand up, The great prince who stands watch over the sons of your people; And there shall be a time of*

trouble, Such as never was since there was a
nation, Even to that time. And at that time
your people shall be delivered, Everyone who
is found written in the book.

I like that verse. At that time, God will have had enough, and Michael is going to stand up. Can you imagine the look on the demon's faces when that happens?

Both verses indicate that Michael has played and will play a major role in events of spiritual warfare. Michael is not alone. Along with Michael stands untold numbers of angels prepared to wage whatever war is necessary at the command of Almighty God. The one thing that is always evident in studying angels is the unquestioning obedience they have for the Father. Like us, they might not have the entire picture or completely understand all aspects of what is going on; but that never matters. They blindly obey and carry out the will of the Father.

Within the framework of our lives is a spiritual war that must be fought. Much of this war takes place in a realm that we cannot see. It is evident from the Bible that the Lord has placed angels in positions to defend the nations of this world from the evils of the dark side. I wonder what angelic battles are taking place on my behalf. This spiritual war that we as Christians face is far greater than you and I have the power to endure on our own. God, in His infinite wisdom, knows this. Remember, He created us and knows our limitations. He also created the angels and knows just how powerful the fallen angels can be. For this reason, He has placed His holy angels around us to assist us in our daily battle against Satan and his minions. Look at the following two verses concerning what the Psalmist says about how the angels surround us in protection.

*The angel of the LORD encamps all around
those who fear Him, And delivers them.*

Psalm 34:7

*For He shall give His angels charge over you,
To keep you in all your ways.*

Psalm 91:11

Both verses reassure us that angels are there behind the scenes. We may not ever see them, but it is reassuring to know that they are there to help us. A word of caution here, angels are not there to deliver us from temptation. It is our job to stand against that. That's why Paul says in Ephesians 6:10-18 for us to put on the armor of God. We must do our part. Remember, this is war. When in battle, it is best to be dressed for war. But we must remember also that the angels are there for our protection and to assist us in doing the will of the Father, not to make personal choices for us. Their battles are on a much greater scale.

So, there you have it. The archangel is the chief of angels. He stands at the head of a mighty angelic army prepared to lead them in whatever the Father commands. His power, intelligence, and wisdom are limited only by God; and he has at his disposal all the resources necessary to carry out the will of the Father. There may be multiple archangels, but the Bible only reveals one. That one is Michael.

CHAPTER ELEVEN

GABRIEL

Out of all the angels in the Bible, there is no doubt that Gabriel is the most famous. In fact, for most people when they think of angels, they inherently think of Gabriel. Maybe this is because of the Christmas story that they have known since childhood, where it is Gabriel that appears to Mary with the good news of Jesus. Or perhaps it stems from a favorite gospel song about Gabriel blowing his horn to announce the return of Christ. Whatever the reason, it seems that the name Gabriel is associated in many minds with angels in general.

Before we get to the specifics about Gabriel, there is one facet about him that we need to clarify. The one title most given to the angel Gabriel is that of an archangel. As mentioned in the previous chapter, the Bible only gives the title archangel to one angel and that angel is Michael. So why would so many people in the world attribute the title of archangel to Gabriel?

The Protestant Bible nor the Catholic Bible specifically give the title archangel to the angel Gabriel. The Catholic Bible in the book of Tobit does however mention seven Holy angels *"which present the prayers of the saints and enter into the presence of the glory of the Holy one."* Tobit 12:15. Traditionally, these seven angels have been considered archangels, of which Gabriel is one. Given that the Catholic Church has had a wide and lasting impression on the culture of people throughout the world, it is easily understandable that a vast majority would also see Gabriel as an archangel. However, one must be careful in making assumptions in scripture. Although Gabriel is traditionally seen by the Catholic Church as an archangel, the Catholic Bible, like the protestant Bible, only specifically gives the title archangel to the angel Michael and no other. In addition, the definition of archangel itself being "the" chief angel, lends credence to the fact that there can only be one archangel. The Bible makes it clear that Michael is that chief angel, not Gabriel.

The name Gabriel means "Mighty one of God". He is known as the angel "who stands in the presence of the Lord." Most of what we know about Gabriel is that his primary purpose is to bring messages and understanding from God to His people.

The first time we see Gabriel in scripture occurs in Daniel chapter 8. Daniel has been saved from the lion's den and goes on to survive and serve several kings. The first year that King Belshazzar was king of Babylon, Daniel began having, over the course of the next several years, a series of dreams and visions about the end times. These visions, found in chapters 7-9, are well worth the time and effort put into reading them and are subjects for many sermons. Suffice it to say here that they were greatly disturbing to Daniel and troubled him. So much so that he says that "my countenance changed".

Gabriel makes his first appearance in verse 15. Daniel has been praying and seeking God's wisdom concerning the meaning of the dreams and visions. Verses 15 through 19 reads.

*Then it happened, when I, Daniel, had seen
the vision and was seeking the meaning, that
suddenly there stood before me one having
the appearance of a man. And I heard a
man's voice between the banks of the Ulai,
who called, and said, "Gabriel, make this
man understand the vision." So he came
near where I stood, and when he came I was
afraid and fell on my face; but he said to me,
"Understand, son of man, that the vision
refers to the time of the end."
Now, as he was speaking with me, I was in
a deep sleep with my face to the ground; but
he touched me, and stood me upright. And he
said, "Look, I am making known to you what
shall happen in the latter time of the indigna-
tion; for at the appointed time the end shall
be.*

Then in the next chapter, chapter 9, we see Gabriel again
coming to Daniel to bring more understanding about his
dreams and visions.

*Now while I was speaking, praying, and
confessing my sin and the sin of my people
Israel, and presenting my supplication before
the LORD my God for the holy mountain
of my God, yes, while I was speaking in
prayer, the man Gabriel, whom I had seen in
the vision at the beginning, being caused to
fly swiftly, reached me about the time of the
evening offering. And he informed me, and
talked with me, and said, "O Daniel, I have*

now come forth to give you skill to under-
stand. At the beginning of your supplications
the command went out, and I have come to
tell you, for you are greatly beloved; there-
fore consider the matter, and understand the
vision:

Daniel chapter 10 tells us that Daniel, through Gabriel's visits, did indeed come to understand the meaning behind the dreams and visions.

Along with the book of Revelation, the book of Daniel records much of what is to take place during the end times. Imagine, if you would, being Daniel. He has never heard of the end times as you and I have today. We have been surrounded by sermons and books concerning those events for most of our lives, but this was all new to Daniel. I would imagine that it was a traumatic experience for him to have these dreams and visions knowing that they were from God, but not understanding their meaning. Gabriel brought that meaning and understanding to Daniel. God sent Gabriel from His very throne room to the place Daniel was, not once but twice, to help him understand. Thanks to those visits from Gabriel and Daniels's obedience to record the visions and dreams, you and I now have a reference as to the things that will take place at some point in the future during the end times.

By the time we hear from Gabriel again, some five hundred years have passed. The Israelites are no longer slaves in the land of Babylon but are living under the thumb of oppression of the Roman Empire in the very land that God promised would always belong to the Israelites. They have returned to Jerusalem where they worship in the temple as God's chosen people.

Part of that worship involved the Holy of Holies. This was the most sacred room in the temple. It was in the innermost part of the temple and was constructed as a perfect square and finely adorned with wood and gold. Inside the Holy of Holies was the Arc of the Covenant, the most sacred symbol of Israel's relationship with God.

The top of the Arc of the Covenant was known as the Mercy Seat. Once a year on the day of atonement, Yom Kippur, a priest was allowed to enter the Holy of Holies and offer a blood sacrifice on the Mercy Seat along with burning incense to atone for the sins of Israel. The honor of entering the Holy of Holies was given to a priest once in his lifetime and the selection was similar to a lottery system. In this particular year, the honor fell on a man named Zachariah or Zacharias depending on your translation.

Zachariah along with his wife Elizabeth were righteous people who lived a life that honored God in everything that they did. He may have been a priest there in Jerusalem or it's possible that he was a priest from a synagogue in a neighboring town. They were an older couple with no children. Like so many women of that time, Elizabeth had never been able to conceive a child. They had long given up hope of having children and were living out their golden years serving God.

While Zachariah was in the Holy of Holies performing his rituals, Gabriel appeared to him. Now think if you will what that must have been like for Zachariah. He is already overwhelmed by simply being allowed to enter the Holy of Holies. I imagine that when he first went in that he probably simply stood there for quite some time just looking around in awe. The next thing he knows is an angel is standing in the Holy of Holies with him. This is a place where no one else is supposed to be. It probably scared him stiff. I'm sure Gabriel thought nothing about it since he is accustomed to being in the very throne room of

God; but, Zachariah was probably a little freaked out. As if simply being in the Holy of Holies with an angel was not enough, Gabriel delivers Zachariah news that is impossible for him to believe. Luke 1:5-25 begins the story.

There was in the days of Herod, the king of Judea, a certain priest named Zacharias, of the division of Abijah. His wife was of the daughters of Aaron, and her name was Elizabeth. And they were both righteous before God, walking in all the commandments and ordinances of the Lord blameless. But they had no child, because Elizabeth was barren, and they were both well advanced in years.

So it was, that while he was serving as priest before God in the order of his division, according to the custom of the priesthood, his lot fell to burn incense when he went into the temple of the Lord. And the whole multitude of the people was praying outside at the hour of incense. Then an angel of the Lord appeared to him, standing on the right side of the altar of incense. And when Zacharias saw him, he was troubled, and fear fell upon him.

But the angel said to him, "Do not be afraid, Zacharias, for your prayer is heard; and your wife Elizabeth will bear you a son, and you shall call his name John. And you will have joy and gladness, and many will rejoice at his birth. For he will be great in the sight of the Lord, and shall drink neither wine nor strong drink. He will also be filled with the Holy Spirit, even from his mother's womb. And he

*will turn many of the children of Israel to the
Lord their God. He will also go before Him
in the spirit and power of Elijah, 'to turn the
hearts of the fathers to the children,' and the
disobedient to the wisdom of the just, to make
ready a people prepared for the Lord."
And Zacharias said to the angel, "How shall
I know this? For I am an old man, and my
wife is well advanced in years."
And the angel answered and said to him, "I
am Gabriel, who stands in the presence of
God, and was sent to speak to you and bring
you these glad tidings. But behold, you will
be mute and not able to speak until the day
these things take place, because you did not
believe my words which will be fulfilled in
their own time."
And the people waited for Zacharias, and
marveled that he lingered so long in the
temple. But when he came out, he could not
speak to them; and they perceived that he had
seen a vision in the temple, for he beckoned to
them and remained speechless.
So it was, as soon as the days of his ser-
vice were completed, that he departed to his
own house. Now after those days his wife
Elizabeth conceived; and she hid herself five
months, saying, "Thus the Lord has dealt
with me, in the days when He looked on me,
to take away my reproach among people."*

At this point, we temporarily take a break from the story of Zachariah and Elizabeth to focus on the story of Mary. It has been six months since Gabriel visited Zachariah and since Elizabeth's conception. The setting is now a little town about sixty miles north of Jerusalem across the Jezreel Valley known as Nazareth. A quaint little town filled not with high priests and rich people, but with normal common Israelites. In this town, we find Mary. A young lady, probably in her teens, engaged to a strong young carpenter named Joseph. God sent Gabriel to this little town to see Mary and deliver news to her that would change all mankind forever. I'll let Luke tell the story.

Now in the sixth month the angel Gabriel was sent by God to a city of Galilee named Nazareth, to a virgin betrothed to a man whose name was Joseph, of the house of David. The virgin's name was Mary. And having come in, the angel said to her, "Rejoice, highly favored one, the Lord is with you; blessed are you among women!" But when she saw him, she was troubled at his saying, and considered what manner of greeting this was. Then the angel said to her, "Do not be afraid, Mary, for you have found favor with God. And behold, you will conceive in your womb and bring forth a Son, and shall call His name JESUS. He will be great, and will be called the Son of the Highest; and the Lord God will give Him the throne of His father David. And He will reign over the house of Jacob forever, and of His kingdom there will be no end." Then Mary said to the angel, "How can this

be, since I do not know a man?"
And the angel answered and said to her,
"The Holy Spirit will come upon you, and
the power of the Highest will overshadow
you; therefore, also, that Holy One who is
to be born will be called the Son of God.
Now indeed, Elizabeth your relative has also
conceived a son in her old age; and this is
now the sixth month for her who was called
barren. For with God nothing will be impos-
sible."
Then Mary said, "Behold the maidservant
of the Lord! Let it be to me according to your
word." And the angel departed from her.

To keep this focused on the angel Gabriel, I'll summarize the rest of the story for you. Elizabeth does indeed give birth to a little boy who is later called John the Baptist; Zachariah regains his ability to speak; and Mary as we know gives birth to our Savior, Jesus Christ.

Some of you know the Christmas story well and are probably thinking that I left out the part about Gabriel appearing to Joseph. You are right. I did leave that out – on purpose. An angel did visit Joseph but listen closely to what the scripture says.

Now the birth of Jesus Christ was as follows:
After His mother Mary was betrothed to
Joseph, before they came together, she was
found with child of the Holy Spirit. Then
Joseph her husband, being a just man, and
not wanting to make her a public example,

was minded to put her away secretly. But
while he thought about these things, behold,
an angel of the Lord appeared to him in a
dream, saying, "Joseph, son of David, do not
be afraid to take to you Mary your wife, for
that which is conceived in her is of the Holy
Spirit. And she will bring forth a Son, and
you shall call His name JESUS, for He will
save His people from their sins."

Did you catch that? Matthew says, *"behold, an angel of the Lord..."* He did not say "behold, Gabriel..." Matthew simply tells us that "an" angel of the Lord came to Joseph. Whenever Gabriel is dispatched throughout the Bible to visit someone, the scripture names him specifically. It does not do so in this case leading scholars to believe that this angel, although an important angel with an important message to bring, was not Gabriel himself but another angel whose name is not given.

Another misconception about Gabriel is that he will be the one to blow the horn announcing the return of Christ. This indeed may be the case, but scripture simply says in 1 Thessalonians 4,

For the Lord Himself will descend from heaven
with a shout, with the voice of an archangel, and
with the trumpet of God.

In the book of Revelation, we do see numerous occasions of angels blowing trumpets, but none mention Gabriel specifically. This idea of Gabriel being the one to blow the horn probably originated from the idea of Gabriel being an archangel as mentioned earlier and from his popularity in scripture. He is the most named angel besides The Angel of the Lord in scripture and as such has become an integral part of folklore and gospel songs. Will it be Gabriel? I don't know, but one day, we will all find out.

Four times we see the angel Gabriel mentioned in the Bible. Each time, he is dispatched from God to either bring understanding and wisdom or to deliver messages and instruction from God. No doubt that Gabriel is an impressive angel. Out of the untold number of angels in heaven, he is specifically mentioned as having the honor and privilege of continuously standing in the presence of God. I can't wait to meet him someday.

CHAPTER TWELVE

LUCIFER

In October of 1347, twelve ships docked in the Sicilian port of Messina. Like any other day when ships arrived, people were there to greet the sailors. Fantasizing about what adventures they had been on as well as curious about what cargo they might have brought, they flocked to the docks for what was ordinarily a happy occasion. But this day was different. When the ships docked, the people were horrified to find that most of the sailors aboard the ships were dead, and the sailors that were alive were on the verge of death themselves. Covered in black, rotten boils that oozed blood and pus, the sailors held on to what life was left. The ships were ordered to leave the harbor, but it was simply too late. The local people became infected with an illness that caused blood and pus to seep out of unusually large and fowl smelling growths. What followed were horrific symptoms of fever, chills, aches, and pains, as well as uncontrollable vomiting and diarrhea. People that went to bed ordinarily healthy would be found dead by morning.

Not long after the sickness devastated Messina, it laid siege to Marseilles, France, and the port cities of Genoa and Venice. Soon after, Pisa, Rome, Florence, Paris, Bordeaux,

Lyon, and London were stricken with the horrific epidemic which continued to spread throughout all of Europe. People fled from any area of the populace to no avail. Even the animals that were depended on daily for food and sustenance were completely overwhelmed. Over the next half-decade, what would become known as the Black Death would end the lives of over 200 million people.

Today, we know the Black Death as a plague that is spread by a bacillus called *Yersina pestis*. Sanitary conditions in the medieval period of this time were lacking or nonexistent. Ships were infested with rats and fleas both of which spread the bacillus through their infectious bites. Because they traveled the world docking in port city after port city, these ships soon became the primary means for the spread of this horrific sickness. Once infected, all that was required to spread the plague was a simple touch or breath.

At the time, no one knew what spread the sickness from one person to another. Many people concluded that what was befalling them was a punishment from God for their heresy, fornication, and several other sins. To rid themselves of this pestilence, they attempted to win favor with God by purging themselves of heretics and other troublemakers. What seemed to be the evilest sickness that had ever fallen on man was soon followed by some of the evilest times in human history. Mass killings, torture, and burning at the stake, became commonplace. Evil followed evil.

This was just one evil epidemic at one particular time in history. I'm sure that the history buffs out there could sit down with pen and paper and list out dozens of events and times in which great evils were displayed by mankind. Events such as the attacks on the World Trade Center on 9-11, the Holocaust, the World Wars that have been fought, the Spanish Inquisition, and so on. Along with this long list of major events could be made an even longer list of minor evils that trouble us and try us daily. This world, as full as it is with good, is brimming over with evil. How could a world, created perfectly by God, contain such evil? The answer whittles down to one fallen angel. His name is Lucifer, or more commonly, Satan.

Most of us have preconceived ideas about Satan, such as what he looks like, where he lives, and so forth. Unfortunately for many, the ideas they have about Satan come from Hollywood's scary movies or some well-meaning adult during their childhood conjuring up horrific notions to make us stay out of trouble. However, like the topics before this one, the only real source of information we have is the Bible; so that's where we will turn. Through the pages of our Bibles, we will learn the truth about Satan, his demons, and our battle against this powerful foe.

Before we dive into the details of Satan, let's review a little about the history of angels. First off, we know that angels are created beings just like you and me. God created them for His purpose and plan. John 1:1-3 tells us that in the beginning was God and that He created all things. Colossians 1:16 says that all things were created through Him. Angels are their own entity as part of God's creation.

Secondly, we know that they were created at some point prior to God creating our universe. God makes this point clear to Job in Job 38:4-7. There we find God asking Job *"Where were you when I laid the foundations of the earth?"* And continues with *"When the morning stars sang together, and all the sons of God shouted for joy?"*

Why are these two facts important? Because to understand Satan, we need to understand where he came from and why he does the things that he does.

Long before he was called Satan, he was known as Lucifer. A name that means "morning star", "son of the dawn", "day star", or "shining star". In Hebrew, he was known as "helel". He was one of the most gorgeous angels in

Heaven, perfect in all his ways, and likely at the top of the angelic hierarchy. Ezekiel tells us more about him in Ezekiel chapter 28.

You were the seal of perfection,
Full of wisdom and perfect in beauty.
You were in Eden, the garden of God;
Every precious stone was your covering:
The sardius, topaz, and diamond,
Beryl, onyx, and jasper,
Sapphire, turquoise, and emerald with gold.
The workmanship of your timbrels and pipes
Was prepared for you on the day you were
created.
"You were the anointed cherub who covers;
I established you;
You were on the holy mountain of God;
You walked back and forth in the midst of
fiery stones.
You were perfect in your ways from the day
you were created,
Till iniquity was found in you.

So, what happened to him? How could an angel, created by God, living in the holiest and perfect place become the vilest creature to ever exist? To answer that, we need to look no further than ourselves. Simply look at history and the things that are going on in our world today. War seems to always be looming on the horizon. Crime is at an all-time high throughout the globe. The love of self has been no greater than it is now. People want what others have and will go to any length to get it. Envy, jealousy, pride, and hatred all seem to be increasing at an alarming rate. We know from the book of Genesis that we humans inherited those traits from Satan in the Garden of Eden. All these traits we exercise with the same free will that God gave to the angels. It was this free will combined with envy, jealousy, pride, and arrogance that changed Lucifer from one of the most prized angels in heaven to the adversary of all who love the Lord. We see this as Ezekiel continues in chapter 28 verses 16-19.

"By the abundance of your trading
You became filled with violence within,
And you sinned;
Therefore I cast you as a profane thing
Out of the mountain of God;
And I destroyed you, O covering cherub,
From the midst of the fiery stones.
"Your heart was lifted up because of your
beauty;
You corrupted your wisdom for the sake of
your splendor;
I cast you to the ground,
I laid you before kings,
That they might gaze at you.
"You defiled your sanctuaries
By the multitude of your iniquities,
By the iniquity of your trading;
Therefore I brought fire from your midst;
It devoured you,
And I turned you to ashes upon the earth
In the sight of all who saw you.
All who knew you among the peoples are
astonished at you;
You have become a horror,
And shall be no more forever."

Lucifer's pride and arrogance got the best of him. His envy and jealousy became an iniquity in him that would cost him everything. Isaiah gets to the core of the matter as he revealed what was in Lucifer's heart.

> *For you have said in your heart:*
> *I will ascend into heaven,*
> *I will exalt my throne above the stars of God;*
> *I will also sit on the mount of the congrega-*
> *tion*
> *On the farthest sides of the north;*
> *I will ascend above the heights of the clouds,*
> *I will be like the Most High.'*

Lucifer decided he wanted to be God. He was arrogant enough to think that he could replace his creator. His thoughts and actions became sinful, and that could not be tolerated in a place that was designed to be sin free. So, God kicked him out of Heaven.

Ezekiel tells us that God "Cast" Lucifer to the ground. He said, *"I cast you to the ground, I laid you before kings, That they might gaze at you."* According to the Merriam-Webster dictionary, to cast means to throw away, get rid of, shed or molt. God didn't simply make Lucifer leave; He threw Lucifer out of heaven banishing him to the ground of Earth. This must have been a memorable day in Heaven. Jesus says it was like watching lightning. Remember, Jesus has always been. He knew Lucifer well and was there the day that he was thrown out of Heaven. He tells His disciples about seeing it in Luke 10:18.

"And He said to them, "I saw Satan fall like lightning from heaven."

This scripture is interesting in that although Jesus knew him as Lucifer in heaven, He calls him Satan here. The name Satan means adversary. That's exactly what Satan is. He is Jesus' adversary. Satan wanted to be God. He wanted to rule all of Heaven and the universe. He knows now that is not going to happen, and that Jesus will be inheriting that kingdom and living the life that Satan always wanted. Therefore, he is an adversary to Jesus. I would go a step further and say that he is also our adversary. Satan will do anything in his power to keep mankind from going to Heaven. He was there. He knows how perfect Heaven is and what life there is like. He also knows that God desires that people live with Him there in perfect peace. Keep in mind that Satan was kicked out of Heaven. He is upset about that, and does not want you or me to fulfill God's plan by living in the very place that he wanted to rule yet was forced to leave. He can't live there, so he does not want you to live there either.

Satan is also referred to in the Bible as the devil. The Greek "diabolos" means slanderer and translates into the word "devil". This goes along with John 8:44 where John refers to him as the "father of lies". To slander is to do no other than lie. It seems that one of Satan's primary tactics is to bend the truth or flat-out lie about what the truth is. His primary targets when it comes to slander are God, Christ, and anything to do with the perfect plan laid out for mankind. He would love to make the entire world believe that they don't need God and salvation at all. So many people in this world today believe that they are going to heaven simply for being good people. After all, if God is so loving, He wouldn't condemn someone to Hell for eternity. At least that's what Satan would have us believe. He used that same tactic with Adam and Eve in the Garden of Eden. *"You will not surely die....."* he said. We all know the rest of the story.

We most commonly refer to Lucifer as the devil. The word "devil" is used throughout the bible and most often refers to Satan himself; however, the plural form of this word, "devils" is often seen and most often refers to Satan's angels or demons. In our modern language, Satan is simply referred to as the devil. Thinking about the word devil conjures up images of some dragon-looking creature with horns on his head, long pointy fingernails, and evil eyes. Hollywood and artists throughout history have done their best to make us believe that this is what Satan looks like. We must keep in mind that Satan is the father of lies. If Satan were to come knocking on your door, he would not appear as some fierce dragon creature ready to devour you. No, he would appear as someone nice to look at, someone that makes you feel easy about yourself. He would appear as someone you feel you could trust. The Bible even calls him the angel of light. He will so trick the world with his artificial beauty, that he'll make even the bad things seem good. He'll convince the world that what is bad is good, what is ugly is beautiful, and what is sinful is not. Look around our world today; it's happening.

We are partly to blame for this change in our world, because we don't fully understand our adversary. We tend to give Satan more credit than he is due. We have been taught our entire lives about him and about how powerful he is. Because of this, we tend to give him attributes that belong only to God. These attributes would be the same three "Omnis" that we discussed earlier when talking about the limitations of angels.

The first of the three omnis is omnipotent. Satan is not omnipotent. Only God is omnipotent. Omnipotent means all-powerful. We tend to think of Satan in this way;

however, only one can be omnipotent, and we know that Satan is not simply by looking at who threw who out of heaven. In addition to this, God revealed to John in the book of Revelation, the "end of the story" if you would. We know through John's vision that Satan is eventually defeated and thrown into the Lake of Fire for all eternity. These two examples alone are enough to show that Satan is not omnipotent and that only God is. However, we tend to give Satan that attribute in our daily battles against sin. We feel beaten before we ever begin to fight. We feel powerless against the dark forces of sin in our lives, and often have the "what's the use, I'm just going to sin again" mentality. That's exactly the attitude Satan wants you to have. Next time that little attitude wants to rear its head into your fight against sin, just remember the only one that is truly omnipotent is the one that is on your side.

The second omni is that of omniscience. Omniscience is being all-knowing. Only God is all-knowing. The Bible tells us that even the angels do not know the day or the hour that the Lord will return. Satan is no more than an angel. This alone demonstrates that he is not all-knowing. He doesn't have a clue when Christ will return, and it scares him to death. He knows enough to know that he is defeated in the end; however, he doesn't know how much time is left before that end. He simply keeps guessing the timing and working as hard and as fast as he can to entrap as many people as possible into his lie before that day comes. It is as simple as this, if Satan were omniscient, he would have known from the start that his little plan to become like God was not going to work.

The last omni is omnipresent. Omnipresent is being in all places at the same time. Hollywood again has helped us to think of Satan in this way. Whenever the night is dark and scary, we tend to think that Satan is lurking in the shadows. Indeed, he may be, but can he be in the dark shadows everywhere simultaneously? The answer is no. Like the Omnis before, only God is omnipresent. In Job 1 we see that God has summoned His angels to give an account of themselves. When Satan comes before God, he was asked *"Where have you come from?"* Satan answered, *"From roaming through the earth and going back and forth in it."* If Satan were omnipresent, he would not need to roam through the earth or go back and forth in it because he would have been everywhere at once.

Like the other angels, Satan is not limited by time and space like you and me, and hence can go from place to place in an instant. Also, like the other angels, he can only be in one place at a particular moment. This brings up an interesting point to ponder. If he can only be in one place at any given moment, then at this very instant his location could be given coordinates. Said another way, at this very moment, Satan has GPS coordinates. With our modern-day Global Positioning Systems, we can pinpoint an object with uncanny precision. The location of an object can be determined within a foot of where it is. Since Satan is not omnipresent, it could be said that his location could be determined, and that one could go to that location and find him there. Why a person would ever want to do that is beyond me. The point here is that Satan cannot be in multiple places at the same time.

Just by looking at the three omnis, we see that Satan is not even close to being on the level with God even though we often attribute God-like traits to him. However, let me say this; his powers far outweigh those possessed by you and me. The Bible makes it clear that angels are superior to humans, and since Satan is an angel, his powers are superior to ours. So, for one to think that they could defeat Satan at his own game is simply fooling themselves into a false sense of security. The beautiful thing about salvation is that we don't have to defeat Satan – he is already defeated.

The Bible refers to Satan as the Prince of this World. Not to worry, John 4:4 tells us.

He who is in you is greater than he who is in the world.

If you are a child of God, then Christ is in you, and He is far greater than any angel that was ever created. When it comes to angels, whether fallen or not, they act under the authority of God. R.C. Sproul said it best in his book *Unseen Realities,*

We need to see that everything that Satan does is always under the sovereign authority of God. Satan can't move a finger without divine permission.

CHAPTER THIRTEEN

FALLEN ANGELS

I recently saw a meme where a terminally ill lady wanted to play a joke on her friends and family. Before she passed away, she had cards made up for each person to receive at her funeral. The front of the card read, "Let's keep in touch." On the inside of the card was a picture of a Ouija board. I must admit when I first saw that I found it comical; but beyond the comedy lies something far more serious.

During the 19th Century, Americans were obsessed with spirituality; especially in the form of communication with the dead. The average lifespan of people at the time was somewhere around 50 years, and the appeal that one could communicate with a loved one that all too soon had left this world drew in followers of all ages and social statuses. It has even been reported that Mary Todd Lincoln, wife of Abraham Lincoln, held a séance in the White House after her 11-year-old son died in 1862. This nationwide obsession with communicating with the dead led to the creation of the Ouija board.

The Ouija board was first advertised for sale in February 1891 as the "Ouija, the Wonderful Talking Board". It would set you back a whole $1.50. The Kennard Novelty Company, the makers of the first Ouija boards, probably didn't have communication with the dead on their minds as much as communicating with the wallets of the American public. The boards were a big hit and people from all over the country bought the boards with the sole purpose of talking with their long-lost loved ones.

On the surface, these boards and talking with the dead might seem harmless and even comical to some; but once you get beyond that, it leaves one with the uneasy feeling of the dark side of the spiritual world. The truth of this sort of thing reveals the stark reality of a demonic presence. If communication takes place, it is not with a long-lost loved one but with a satanic creature disguising itself as that loved one. Make no mistake about it, when you leave this world, you leave all forms of communication with this world behind. This is not my opinion but is a fact found in the Bible. However, people claim to have had communication with the dead. There may have been communication, but it was not communication with the dead, but communication with an angel; a fallen angel.

Lucifer had made up his mind that he wanted to replace God as the ruler of all heaven and earth. He was convinced that he not only deserved the position, but could obtain it through his influence over the other angels in Heaven. He no doubt made his case with any angel that would listen to him. In his mind, he probably reasoned that if he could win over the other angels then the Lord would have no choice but to step aside and allow him to sit on the throne of Heaven.

We know from scripture that God did not tolerate this behavior in His heavenly realm and promptly kicked Lucifer out of heaven. In addition, we see from scripture that God also kicked out all the angels that had fallen to Lucifer's influence. Revelation 12:3-4 speaks of this.

*And another sign appeared in heaven:
behold, a great, fiery red dragon having seven
heads and ten horns, and seven diadems on
his heads. His tail drew a third of the stars of
heaven and threw them to the earth.*

Nowhere in the Bible does it say specifically that a third of "angels" were cast out of Heaven. However, we know from our previous studies, that angels were represented in Biblical literature as stars. So how can we be sure that the stars mentioned here were angels? For the answer to that, we need to look further into Revelation 12, specifically verses 7-9.

*And war broke out in heaven: Michael and
his angels fought with the dragon; and the
dragon and his angels fought, but they did
not prevail, nor was a place found for them
in heaven any longer. So the great dragon
was cast out, that serpent of old, called the
Devil and Satan, who deceives the whole
world; he was cast to the earth, and his
angels were cast out with him.*

Notice what it says. *"he was cast to the earth, and his angels were cast out with him."* It is clear here that Satan was cast to the Earth and that it was truly angels that were cast out with him. From these two sets of scripture, we can interpret that it was angels that were cast out of heaven with Satan and not just one or two, but a third of them. A third of all the angels in heaven were cast out.

How many is a third? We have already talked in previous chapters about the number of angels and determined that we don't know how many angels God created. It's probably a number far greater than we can fathom. This in turn means that we cannot identify the number that was cast out. Is the actual number important in the big scheme of things anyway? Absolutely not. Suffice it to say that there are plenty and even if there were only one, it would be enough to disrupt the lives of most humans.

Let's take a minute to think about where these many fallen angels might be. In our previous chapter, we talked about the fact that as an angel Satan is not omnipresent. He cannot be in more than one place at any given instant. Satan is merely an angel, despite how some give him more credit than he is due. This means that his angels, whom we refer to as demons, are not omnipresent either. Thus, they cannot be in more than one place at any given instant no more than Satan can. Why is this important? Because we need to realize that even though Satan might not be in our local area at this moment, it does not mean that his angels are not. They work for him. He sends them out with the power to disrupt as many lives as they can. With us not knowing how many there are, we must assume that they are all around us each moment of every day. We can see this verified by simply turning on the evening news. Most of what we see there are stories of people being murdered, spreading hatred, stealing, destroying, etc. When was the last time you saw a newscast of mostly good things?

Remember, Satan wants to destroy your life, your children's lives, as well as the lives of the rest of your friends and family. In short, he wants to destroy everything good under Heaven. He is mad and intends to destroy and disrupt God's plan. He knows that God's plan includes the restoration of His creation at some point in the future. He also knows that this restoration will be the end for him and all his evil demons. In addition, Satan knows that the restoration of creation comes through Jesus Christ. Therefore, from the first moment that Satan fell to the Earth, he has been scheming ways to disrupt God's unstoppable plan.

To see how some Bible scholars believe Satan worked to derail God's plan, let's turn to an unlikely passage in the front of your Bible – Genesis 6:1-8

Now it came to pass, when men began to multiply on the face of the earth, and daughters were born to them, that the sons of God saw the daughters of men, that they were beautiful; and they took wives for themselves of all whom they chose.
And the LORD said, "My Spirit shall not strive with man forever, for he is indeed flesh; yet his days shall be one hundred and twenty years." There were giants on the earth in those days, and also afterward, when the sons of God came in to the daughters of men and they bore children to them. Those were the mighty men who were of old, men of renown.
Then the LORD saw that the wickedness of man was great in the earth, and that every intent of the thoughts of his heart was only evil continually. And the LORD was sorry that He had made man on the earth, and He was grieved in His heart. So the LORD said, "I will destroy man whom I have created from the face of the earth..."

You'll no doubt recognize this as the beginning of the story of Noah's Ark. We all know the story. Mankind becomes evil, God wishes that He had never created mankind and decides to wipe man from the face of the earth. But God finds favor in Noah and directs Noah to build an ark in which He saves Noah and his family from certain death while the rest of mankind and all the animals are destroyed by a flood. Then, the earth is repopulated through the lineage of Noah and his sons.

Why was it that God needed to destroy mankind completely? The Bible tells us that it is because man had become so evil. They had indeed become evil; but have you ever stopped to think about why? The answer, I believe is hidden right before our eyes. An answer that demonstrates that from the beginning Satan knew of God's intent to restore His creation and that He intended to do it through His son Jesus.

Make no mistake about it, Satan desires to turn us all evil. However, at this point in history, he had a specific purpose in mind for doing it. Let's look back at Genesis 6:1-4 again.

Now it came to pass, when men began to multiply on the face of the earth, and daughters were born to them, that the sons of God saw the daughters of men, that they were beautiful; and they took wives for themselves of all whom they chose.
And the LORD said, "My Spirit shall not strive with man forever, for he is indeed flesh; yet his days shall be one hundred and twenty years." There were giants on the earth in those days, and also afterward, when the sons of God came in to the daughters of

men and they bore children to them. Those
were the mighty men who were of old, men of
renown.

We established in a previous chapter that references to
"the Sons of God" were references to angels. The angels
that were kicked out of heaven were sent where? To Earth.
These satanic fallen angels, whom we call demons, were
roaming about the earth while humans were just getting
a good start on populating the planet. Satan knows that
God intends to redeem His creation through His son Jesus
and that Jesus' lineage must be traceable back to Adam,
the first of God's human creation. He also knows that to
redeem mankind and creation, Jesus must be fully human.
So, what better way to derail God's plan than to completely
undo humanity by creating a race of homo-sapiens that
are part human and part angel? If all of mankind becomes
this new genetically altered creature, then there would be
no chance of Jesus being born. After all, Jesus could not be
born to a human that was satanically corrupted in that way.

So, what does he do? He directs his satanic angels to
have sex with human women to change the bloodline of
humanity. This resulted in homo-sapiens that were not fully
human, and a race that became so vile and evil that God
decided that they must be destroyed. The Bible even mentions that this new race of man became giants compared
to other men. Even though the Bible does not mention it
specifically, I can only imagine the other alterations that
must have taken place both outwardly and inwardly in this
new race of people. The only way to stop this perverted
new bloodline and put an end to the evil that was taking
place on the earth at the time was to destroy it simply and
completely. We can be thankful for Noah in that he and
his family stayed true to God through it all.

But what about the fallen angels? What happened to them? I mean, they could not be destroyed by a flood, since as an angel, they don't occupy space and time as we do. For the answer to that question, we need to look to the back of the Bible in the book of Jude.

And the angels who did not keep their proper domain, but left their own abode, He has reserved in everlasting chains under darkness for the judgment of the great day;

Jude tells us that God incarcerated these angels and bound them in chains. They are sentenced to this incarceration for all time until the great judgment.

Clearly, not all the angels that fell from heaven participated in this unsuccessful plan of Satan's and became incarcerated by God. Remember when we talked about Michael the Archangel? We looked at Daniel chapter 10 and found that God dispatched him to help the angel that appeared to Daniel. Let's look at that scripture again for a moment.

But the prince of the kingdom of Persia withstood me twenty-one days; and behold, Michael, one of the chief princes, came to help me, for I had been left alone there with the kings of Persia.

Daniel 10:13

Michael was not dispatched to fight against men, he was dispatched to fight against fallen angels. We need to understand that some of these fallen angels that work so diligently for Satan are assigned the task of interfering with the governing of the nations of this world. Look around at some of the countries on our planet and see how evil those governments have become. History demonstrates this well. Look at Hitler's Germany for instance. Any observer of history can clearly see how evil Hitler's plan was. Only a human that has fallen under a demonic influence could ever dream of, much less pull off the atrocities that Hitler did. Not only did the demons influence Hitler's mind, but influenced enough minds in the German population to turn those evil thoughts into reality resulting in the death of somewhere between 15 and 31 million people. Over a million of which were children who died at the hands of Nazi soldiers. Hitler even told his right-hand man Himmler that it was not enough for the Jews to die; they must die in agony. Evil like this could only come from one source, and that source is Satan and his demonic army.

But Hitler's Germany of World War II is just one example. We could go back through the pages of history and see example after example of times and places where fallen angels have worked to disrupt nations and people from every corner of the globe. We could spend page after page looking at examples of Satanic disruption to governments and in the individual lives of people from all walks of life and probably only scratch the surface. In fact, in the first three books of the New Testament alone, demons are mentioned over 31 times. On and on we could go.

All this talk of Satan, demons, and evil makes the Ouija board sound like child's play. Are we to be on the lookout for demonic forces in our world? Absolutely. Are we to recognize that those forces are there and that their goal is to disrupt and deceive as many people as possible? Absolutely. Are we to fear the fallen angels and tremble in our boots at the mere mention of them? Absolutely not!

Jesus encountered many demons during His earthly ministry. Every single demon that He encountered knew exactly who He was and feared him. He drove them out of possessed people simply using words alone. As one of my professors used to say, "It is blatantly obvious to the most casual observer…" that demons are no match for the Son of God.

Here's the good news. If you are a born-again Christian, you are a child of God. As such, you fall under the protection of God Almighty Himself. Psalm 91:1 says,

He who dwells in the secret place of the Most High shall abide under the shadow of the Almighty.

Can the fallen angels disrupt your life and make things hard on you? Sure, they can; but remember this very important point. Nothing, including fallen angels, can touch your life that has not already passed through the hand of God. Therefore, we should have respect for the power that the fallen angels have and the potential evil that they could inflict on our lives, but fear… we have no need to fear them. At some point in the future when the Day of Judgement arrives, every one of those fallen angels, including Satan, will bow their knee to Jesus. Then just as the Bible predicts, they will be cast into the Lake of Fire where they will remain for all eternity.

CONCLUSION

There will come a day for all of us, as believers, as Christians, as children of God, when we leave this world and step into eternity through the gates of heaven. On that glorious day, we will see for ourselves the beauty of all the marvelous things that God has created that we know little or nothing about. The Bible tells us in 1 Corinthians 2:9,

But as it is written:
"Eye has not seen, nor ear heard,
Nor have entered into the heart of man
The things which God has prepared for those
who love Him."

One of the things that we will see that I imagine will leave us in awe will be the angels. There, we will not only see them, but get to know them, have conversations with them, learn from them, praise God with them, and do who knows what else with them for all eternity.

I pray that you are looking forward to that day with confidence as well. If you are reading this and are not sure if that is in your future, I encourage you to open your heart to Christ and accept Him as your personal savior. The Bible tells us that He is the only way to Heaven and eternal life in the sweet presence of our Lord.

Thank you for allowing me to share with you the things I learned about angels. This book was born out of my curiosity about them. I wanted to know more about them and to share what I learned with those closest to me. As much as I learned, I feel that I have just scratched the surface of who angels are and what they were created to do. It is my hope and prayer that through these pages you have found the answers to questions you might have had about angels and that you learned something new about these magnificent beings just as I have.

May the Lord bless and keep you.

Made in the USA
Columbia, SC
11 October 2023

24288841R00098